EASING
THE PASSAGE

EASING
THE
PASSAGE

A Guide for Prearranging and Ensuring a Pain-Free and
Tranquil Death via a Living Will, Personal Medical Mandate,
and Other Medical, Legal, and Ethical Resources

by
David E. Outerbridge
and
Alan R. Hersh, M.D.

HarperPerennial
A Division of HarperCollinsPublishers

A hardcover edition of this book was published in 1991 by HarperCollins Publishers.

HarperCollins books may be purchased for educational, business, or sales promotional use. For information, please call or write: Special Markets Department, HarperCollins Publishers, Inc., 10 East 53rd Street, New York, NY 10022. Telephone: (212) 207-7528; Fax: (212) 207-7222.

Designed by Barbara DuPree Knowles

THE LIBRARY OF CONGRESS HAS CATALOGUED THE HARDCOVER EDITION AS FOLLOWS:

Outerbridge, David.
  Easing the passage: a guide for prearranging and ensuring a painfree and tranquil death via a living will, personal medical mandate, and other medical, legal, and ethical resources/by David E. Outerbridge, Alan R. Hersh.—1st ed.
    p. cm.
  Includes index.
  ISBN 0-06-016323-2
  1. Right to die—United States. 2. Right to die—Law and legislation—United States. 3. Euthanasia—Social aspects—United States.
I. Hersh, Alan R., 1951– . II. Title.
R726.O93   1991
362.1′75—dc20   90-55937

ISBN 0-06-092157-9 (pbk.)
92 93 94 95 96 RRD 10 9 8 7 6 5 4 3 2 1

A parting gift to my body:
just when it wishes,
I'll breathe my last.

—death poem of the
Japanese Haiku poet
ENSEI, *in 1725*

Contents

Contents

Preface

This book is the collaboration of two authors: one a family physician, the other a journalist. On occasion, it is necessary to speak individually. In those instances, the change in voices is indicated by parenthetical notation, "(Hersh)" or "(Outerbridge)."

Because we want this book to be *read*, it is written in a narrative style that avoids footnotes and other formats that typically encumber medical writings.

The events, legal and medical, that both support and obstruct easing the passage are changing rapidly. Because many of these changes are the product of individual state law (and all fifty states are active on this subject in their legislatures and court systems), some of the data are going to change, even before this book is published. The basic principles, however, will remain in force, and we have identified sources a reader can refer to for guidance on local regulations.

Easing the Passage is not an editorial on the court cases and the right-to-die debate that are filling the news. It is a book of advocacy. Who is to be the spokesperson who ensures that death will take place in a tranquil manner? Who is to protect us? The answer is: Each and every person must do it for themselves and their kin.

Although each of us was involved with the subject of easing the passage professionally—medically and journalistically—before we began this book, neither of us had executed a Living Will or taken the other steps we later learned of and have outlined in this book.

We have rectified this omission and have taken the steps to ensure an eased passage not only for ourselves but also for all immediate family and an ever-growing circle of friends and acquaintances with whom we have discussed the book. (In fact, we have had to deal with a minor frenzy for Xeroxed copies of the manuscript.) Such is the wish for easing the passage and for the means to achieve it that we now believe the counsel contained in this book may be a trigger to a self-fulfilling hope: we come into the world crying but hope to leave it with a smile.

EASING
THE PASSAGE

CHAPTER ONE

An Introduction

What is life? It is the flash of a firefly in the night. It is the breath of a buffalo in the winter time. It is the little shadow which runs across the grass and loses itself in the Sunset.

—the last words of CROWFOOT,
great orator of the Blackfoot Nation

T his is a slender book, but its subject pertains to every living person. It is slender by intent. There are libraries of books that examine death from any number of perspectives: religion, medicine, law, bereavement, metaphysics. *Easing the Passage* duplicates none of those works. It was written with a single purpose: to guide a reader through four—and only four—steps:

1 Acknowledgment of the inevitability of death
2 Appreciation of the universal wish to die peacefully or in one's sleep
3 Examination of the present-day obstacles to a tranquil death
4 Arrival at the solution to these obstacles

Death is a somber event that causes family and friends sadness and loss. It is often made far more distressing for survivors, however, when they are witness to a "bad death," to say nothing of the possible mental and physical pain of the dying patient. *This is avoidable.* "Bad" and "good" are clumsy descriptors for death but are perhaps more accessible than the Greek word *euthanasia* (which has also taken on a new meaning). In the meaning of this book, a good death is one that is free of pain and terror. Unfortunately, there are today

1

many unnecessary bad deaths. It need not be so. *Easing the Passage* is a guide to achieving a good death, which hereafter is referred to as a tranquil death. We choose "tranquil death" over "death with dignity" because the latter is overused and may carry other connotations.

Everyone *wants* a tranquil death, but because people rarely confront their own mortality, they postpone taking the steps that are essential to ensuring it. Before starting this book, readers are invited to answer the following three questions as a test of whether they have provided for easing the passage to a tranquil death.

• Have you executed a Living Will and given a copy of it to your physician?
• Have you assigned a Durable Power of Attorney for Health Care, designating someone to act as your agent in case you are unable to communicate your wishes about health care yourself?
• Have you arranged for your relatives to take the above two steps?

Unless the answer to each of these questions is yes, a reader is walking into the trap of "It isn't going to happen . . . or at least not yet." Remember the story of Damocles. The ancient Greek courtier was seated at a banquet beneath a sword that was suspended over his head by a single hair. The hair may not break soon, but the possibility is present for anyone at any time.

Understanding the four steps—accepting mortality, acknowledging the universal wish for a tranquil death, examining the obstacles, and finding solutions—will provide for a tranquil death within current medical and legal practice. It will clear the dying process of much unnecessary patient and family distress, leaving the sorrow that follows unsullied by anger and frustration. At the same time this book emphasizes the right to a tranquil death, it affirms life and never advocates the "duty to die."

2

Easing the Passage is intended to further conversation and understanding of procedures attendant to the process of dying, but it is hoped there may be an ancillary benefit. By and large, we cannot know *when* we are going to die. If we acknowledge the inevitability of death and take steps to prearrange a pain-free and peaceful death, however, we can extend life's pleasures. We accomplish this in two ways. First, we eliminate the substantial psychological baggage of fear. The primary fear about death, according to a recent survey, is that the process of dying will be accompanied by unmitigated pain. Second, by accepting the concept of our mortality we can live fully so that at the time of death we are spared the tragedy of incompleteness.

The prescriptions in this book are directed principally to adults. This is because much of the decision-making explored in this book is based on the concepts of "informed consent" and "autonomy." Therefore, while the more general principles of easing the passage apply to dying children, a guardian has different responsibilities for a child than for himself.

Easing the Passage presents information so that readers can act on their own behalf or that of a dying relative. The actions recommended are the same for both categories, even if time and circumstance differ.

The title of the book is taken from a phrase in old-time country doctoring in a day when a person bedridden with an incurable affliction was usually at home. The country doctor came by to minister to discomfort. His satchel contained few of today's arsenal of medications. He could not cure tuberculosis, meningitis, diphtheria, or a host of diseases we can control today. He most certainly did not know about most of the modern procedures that can prolong life today. Instead, he dispensed opiates to soothe the mind, dull the pain, and, in the parlance, ease the passage from life to death.

CHAPTER TWO

Acknowledgment
of Mortality

T wo million people die in the United States each year, which works out to more than five thousand every day. Because most people die of chronic illnesses, four million people are actually in the dying process in this country right now, or on the average eleven thousand either die or know that they are dying every single day. There are, in addition, perhaps ten thousand people who are not in the process of dying, but are living in a persistent vegetative state. (*Persistent* is the medical term, but *permanent* is the normal lay word. "Persistent" differs only because it allows for some future medical breakthrough that could restore cognitive behavior.)

This book is for every one of those people this year and for every reader who will contribute to those statistics in years to come. Almost everyone knows of someone who is dying, and by the time we reach middle age most of us have to confront at least the *approach* of death for our parents. When we were young we may have experienced the death of our grandparents, but that probably did not equip us with a strong sense of mortality. Only when we get the news that a mother or father has died are we suddenly smacked with the presence of death. And only if that death has been the conclusion to a lengthy illness are we likely to have had a firsthand experience of the dying *process*.

That, of course, is a broad generalization because the tragedy of an "untimely" death—death that comes unexpectedly through accident or mortal disease—is also part of many families' stories. As a rule, however, in the United States today, where the average life span is more than seventy years, we are in our fifties before we become personally close to death and dying. And perhaps even then death may be perceived as an aberration in a life so concentrated on living. Only in advanced age, when our bodies start showing signs of wear, do we begin to contemplate the prospect of living on without the mate of a lifetime or a dear friend. Then, too, we begin to consider our own demise.

Although it is the single irrefutable consequence of being born, death is surprisingly invisible except in the small print of obituary pages. When we go for a walk in the woods, we hear the songs of countless birds, and we see signs of rabbits, chipmunks, and other small mammals. When we visit a national park we are in the habitat of deer, bear, and fox. Most of these animals have a short life span, but although the woods are visibly full of the living, we rarely see a dead creature. What should be literally death underfoot is nowhere to be found. Nature has eliminated the signs, even the bones and feathers. In his wonderful book, *The Lives of a Cell*, Lewis Thomas wrote of one example of nature's housecleaning:

> Animals seem to have an instinct for performing death alone, hidden. Even the largest, most conspicuous ones find ways to conceal themselves in time. If an elephant missteps and dies in an open place, the herd will not leave him there; the others will pick him up and carry the body from place to place, finally putting it down in some inexplicably suitable location. When elephants encounter the skeleton of an elephant out in the open, they methodically take up each of the bones and distribute them, in a ponderous ceremony, over neighborhood acres.
>
> It is a natural marvel. All of the life of the earth dies, all of the time, in the same volume as the new life that dazzles us each morning, each spring. All we see of this is the odd stump, the fly struggling on the porch floor of the summer house in October.

No one has ever lived who has not died or lives now who will not die. Death is universal. "I will die, as a matter of *fact."* Every human being comes into the world unable to survive independently in the early years. Every human being, including the rich and famous, cries as a baby, eats and defecates, develops ailments, ages. And the heart muscle of every human being sooner or later ceases to operate. (During the time it took to read this paragraph more than one hundred people died of natural causes somewhere in the world.)

Death is the great equalizer. In life, death is our common denominator: the person at the other end of the phone, the person whose birthday is being celebrated, the neighbor, the boss, the wife, the uncle, like ourself, will die.

Although death is universal, it is also intensely personal. For the individual it is the end of life. For the people that care for that individual, death creates a time of grief and bereavement. A number of books describe ways to deal with the sense of loss. For the deceased, however, there is no more difficulty. For the body comes the evolution into ashes or dust. At a higher level, the deceased lives on in the memories of others and in lasting influences given to the family and community. A few are remembered by great work—art, music, philosophy, and invention being tangible portions of their posterity.

It has been said that *it is not death but dying that is hard.* Death creates sorrow for the family, but it is *dying*—a process that usually extends over time—that can be an experience of compounded miseries. *Easing the Passage* is a compendium of steps that, if followed, will minimize or even eliminate those miseries.

First, however, *a person must acknowledge that at some point he or she will die.* This acknowledgment must be of sufficient conviction that a number of steps are taken. Not later, but now. The largest cause of death for people under the age of forty-five is unanticipated accident. For all of those killed by accident, another group survives in a persistent vegetative state: the body was not killed but the brain functions that create personality were. Nancy Cruzan was such a person, and any complacency should be shattered by her story.

THE STORY OF NANCY CRUZAN

Nancy Cruzan was a healthy vivacious woman in her early twenties when she was involved in a serious automobile accident in January 1983. She was thrown from her car and landed facedown in the dirt, unconscious. About fifteen minutes later paramedics arrived at the scene and were able to restart her heart and breathing. In the intervening time, her brain was deprived of oxygen, permanently damaging significant portions. Despite her brain damage, the brain stem—that part of the organ that controls heart and lung functions—continued to work. Until her death seven years later in December 1990, Nancy Cruzan never regained consciousness.

Cruzan was in a persistent vegetative state. Her face was bloated, her eyes rolled randomly, and her limbs were contracted. "Twenty years ago, Nancy would have died that night," says her sister, "but modern medicine stepped in and pulled her back. So now what we would like to see is medicine step out and let her go." Her family asked that artificial life support be withdrawn and that she be allowed to die.

The Missouri Supreme Court said in a four-to-three decision: "The State's interest is not in quality of life. The State's interest is an unqualified interest in life." When this decision was appealed, the U.S. Supreme Court in a five-to-four vote on June 25, 1990, ruled that because Cruzan had left no "clear and convincing evidence" that she would not wish to continue life in this condition, she had to be kept alive.

In September 1990, based on new evidence, the state of Missouri reversed its decision, indicating that it would not object to withdrawal of the feeding tube if so ordered by a judge. Such an order was obtained; the feeding tube was removed; and Nancy Cruzan died on December 26, 1990. Had the decision remained unchanged, so might have Cruzan. She could have lived with artificial tube feeding for another thirty years (at a cost of $130,000 a year), never recovering from her persistent vegetative state.

The court decisions were heartbreaking news for a family that was tortured by seeing a daughter in a pitiful condition it knew she would never have chosen—and once said as much. Such scenarios will be repeated again and again, unless people make clear their wishes in advance (see chapter 5). For Nancy Cruzan there was a solution, however late it came. The point here is that the possibility of death, or near death, is not something just for the elderly population. *It should be the concern of everyone, but will not become so until everyone accepts the fact of their mortality.* (Nancy Cruzan's story has had one beneficial effect: through media coverage of the case, people have been confronted with the issue, and some have taken action. In Atlanta alone, more than three thousand residents paralyzed the local health agency after a phone number as a source for Living Wills was made available. This demand for Living Wills, spurred by the Cruzan story, was repeated in many other communities.)

The current denial of death is perhaps most clearly revealed in our society by a single fact: two out of three people in the United States die intestate, that is, without having written a will. This lack cannot be due to the difficulty of writing a will. Although a lawyer is often helpful in drawing up a will that makes disposition of property to heirs legally clear and that has minimal tax consequences for its beneficiaries, simple wills are available from stationery stores and even come ready-made on inexpensive software for home computers. People fail to write wills because death remains in the hazy distant future and is not considered an imminent possibility.

Easing the Passage is not a book of counsel about wills. Anyone who dies without a will, however, is creating an unnecessary burden for surviving loved ones. Without a will, a person's estate is turned over to anonymous court personnel for administration. Not only is this expensive in fees, it results in decisions that may not be at all what the deceased would have wished. This becomes perhaps most unfortunate in the case of minors. If parents are killed in an accident without a will, how their child is raised is decided by a court-appointed functionary.

Although everyone is vaguely aware that death is *somewhere* in the future, we treat death as taboo in conversation with aging relatives and we do not confront our own mortality.

The subject of death has gone through a long cycle of public and private acceptance and denial. Traditionally, in earlier times, death was an open subject. This was because it was *visible:* death occurred at home. Childhood death was common, and with an extended family living closely together, grandparents, parents, and other relatives were all tended to at home in their final days. It was as much a part of life as the subsequent funeral procession to the family graveyard. Although death was mysterious—and religions and philosophies wrestled with explanations of it—it was a natural and present part of human experience.

More recently the time of dying that once joined families and friends, however, has become a point of separation. The ailing individual is removed from home and isolated in institutions where paid surrogates oversee the dying process. This change has a number of causes. Because we have a mobile and dispersed familial structure today, we are likely to be geographically distant from an ailing relative. Moreover, medicine has become complicated, and we are given to abdicating care and decisions about the care to specialists. It is both the cause and the effect of a denial of death. One historian has called our bias "the pornography of death," arguing that in Victorian times death was an open subject but sex was pornographic. We have reversed the distinction.

Thus, for many, dying has become a lonely process; while they are dying, we fail those we love: at the time companionship is most needed, it is not there. The natural response to this surviving guilt is further avoidance of the subject of death. It is akin to a stream with an obstruction in the middle.

The water flows as a single body, then it divides to go around the obstruction, rejoining on the downstream side. In our culture the dying process (and sometimes old age) is the obstruction. We were together as a family, but we avoid the unpleasantness and unify again afterward at the funeral. Because we are less exposed to the physical presence of death, the process of dying has become one that is too raw to watch.

There is a certain irony in this. We read of mass death in newspapers and see it on television: fatal automobile accidents, plane crashes, fires, famines, wars. They seldom trigger repulsing mechanisms. Furthermore, we delight in the storytelling arts that reveal death. Tragic death is a box-office smash at theaters and opera houses around the world. Personal death, however—the dying relative or friend for whom we could have a constructive role in easing the passage—we avoid.

The medical profession bears some blame for death's taboo quality. Physicians are just beginning to be open with patients on the subject. When Elisabeth Kübler-Ross first asked for access to terminally ill patients, physicians were outraged. That was only twenty-five years ago. Kübler-Ross's credentials were in order. Why, then, the refusal? Perhaps because physicians themselves do not receive training in dealing with death. Their entire curriculum is centered on *preventing* death. Being human, also, physicians must deal with personal responses to confronting their own mortality with each dying patient.

In *Celebrations of Death*, authors Richard Huntington and Peter Metcalf studied funeral customs in a number of areas, from highly developed societies to primitive tribal cultures and from ancient to modern times. Their principal finding when looking at our own funeral practice was that although the United States is a highly heterogeneous society with many closely held ethnic differences, its peoples tend to manage their funerals in a uniform way: a rapid disappearance of the body into the charge of a funeral director, who executes a series of actions: embalming and cosmetic touch-up (to give the deceased a more *lifelike* appearance); a brief viewing, which many people avoid (a further denial); and an expeditious burial. These funeral practices are another shelter erected against an association with death, and the funeral director has become the family's surrogate in dispatching the evidence of death.

Rather suddenly the trends are changing once again, and the taboo quality of death as a subject is lifting. Death is coming out of the closet. Within the past three years various national media have placed the enigma of death on the front page and on prime time. The right to die was a cover story for *Time;* more than once court cases about whether to let people die made the front page of the *New York Times* and other major dailies; PBS ran a six-hour documentary called "Near Death"; and "death with dignity" was a featured theme on a number of national television programs.

In general, this is a salutary trend. There are, however, two worrisome accompaniments to the ballooning discussion of death. The first is the very reason it has become a topic of debate: it is due to the fact that medical technology has a newfound ability to intrude on the natural dying process and artificially extend it. (This is discussed in chapter 4.) The second troublesome side effect is that in the flash of exposure to the subject due to mass communication, death has climbed the hit parade chart of politics. There is a danger that easing the passage, which should be a *personal* matter between an individual, family, and physician, will be legislated into a set of generic rules about what can and cannot be done. It has even become mixed into the abortion argument. The right-to-life argument in the abortion debate essentially centers on the issue of whether one or two lives are involved. Anti-abortionists argue that the fetus is a human being from the instant of conception and therefore a life that cannot be terminated by abortion. In the case of an individual in a terminal or persistent vegetative state, this debate is inappropriate because an adult has the right to autonomy in choosing or rejecting medical treatment. Nonetheless, among the abortion foes are advocates for the position that medicine should not be allowed to shorten a life even if as an unintended but foreseen consequence of such things as pain control. Opponents of the right to abortion connect the two issues by means of a premise that the *Roe v. Wade* decision—which legalized abortion—is given strength by a patient's right to forego artificial life support (thus implicitly giving credence to a human right over life and death). And their language is becoming strident: "The most horrible story of the twenty-first century" was one label applied to the movement for the right to die.

If the subject of death is becoming less taboo and more open, it has not yet translated into a widespread *personal* acknowledgment of mortality. The universal wish for a tranquil death can become a reality, however, only when we personally accept our mortality. The sword of Damocles hangs over us all.

CHAPTER THREE

Aladdin's Wish, Updated

As the Bible teaches, the road which opens
with birth leads to the grave. Birth and death
are the most singular events we experience,
and therefore the contemplation of death as
of birth should be a thing of beauty and not
ignobility.
—SENATOR JACOB JAVITS testifying before the
House Select Committee on Aging*

In *Tales from the Arabian Nights*, a young man, Aladdin,
finds an old lamp. On his polishing it, a genie emerges from
the spout. The genie, in thanks for being released from cap-
tivity, offers to grant Aladdin a series of wishes. In the literature of folktales, which contain many parallel stories, the
wish is usually for the hand of the beautiful princess, eternal
youth, or a fortune of gold.

In the real world, it is everyone's wish that they die peacefully in their sleep when the time comes. The story of Aladdin
is fiction, but the real-world wish can be granted, at least
metaphorically. If dying in one's sleep means dying without
pain, terror, and ignobility—what this book describes as a
tranquil death—the junction of that hope and the means to
achieve it can be arranged.

We cannot choose *when* we will die. Unfortunately most
deaths come too soon—the result of a sudden accident or fatal
affliction—or too late—after a long, debilitating chronic illness. Modern medicine can, however, control circumstances
to ease the passage of someone with terminal illness or who is
in a persistent vegetative state.

* At the time he testified, Senator Javits was paralyzed from the neck down and was
dying, a situation that, he remarked, "concentrates the mind on this subject."

Although modern medicine cannot legally actively expedite death by a lethal dosage (murder), it is legal, ethical, and recognized as acceptable medical practice to allow a natural series of events to take place that will result in death.

The American Medical Association's Council on Ethical and Judicial Affairs has made this statement for the guidance of physicians:

> The social commitment of the physician is to sustain life and relieve suffering. Where the performance of one duty conflicts with the other, the preference of the patient should prevail. . . . For humane reasons, with informed consent, a physician may do what is medically necessary to alleviate severe pain, or cease or omit treatment to permit a terminally ill patient to die when death is imminent. . . . Even if death is not imminent but a patient is beyond doubt permanently unconscious, and there are adequate safeguards to confirm the accuracy of the diagnosis, it is not unethical to discontinue all means of life-prolonging medical treatment.
>
> Life-prolonging medical treatment includes medication and artificially or technologically supplied respiration, nutrition or · hydration. In treating a terminally ill or permanently unconscious patient, the dignity of the patient should be maintained at all times.

However, as is discussed in chapter 4, interference with the natural dying process is also largely medical. This interference is what impels some seven thousand aging people to commit suicide each year in this country. (The rate of suicide in the over-sixty-five age group is increasing by 25 percent.)

As indicated in chapter 1, *Easing the Passage* considers only four progressive steps: acknowledgment of mortality, the universal wish for a tranquil death, the present-day obstacles to that wish, and the solution to the obstacles. This chapter on the universal wish is surprisingly short. Its brevity, however, merely testifies to the simplicity and clarity of the wish; it can be granted.

CHAPTER 4

Why It Goes Wrong: The Obstacles

The fear of *not* dying during sleep but of persisting in a living hell of dying is not misplaced in the norm of terminal care today. One recurring tragedy is that of elderly people who, fearing lonely, painful, terror-filled deaths, hoard sleeping pills that they can take to preempt a lingering and hard death. Because most medications have a limited shelf-life efficacy or will be rejected by the stomach in massive doses, these suicide attempts often fail. "Because I don't fear death but do fear dying, I think often about suicide. I would like to have at hand a humane method of becoming dead," wrote one university professor. The central goal of this book is to ensure a predetermined sequence of events so that fear of a difficult death is replaced with confidence of an eased passage. *Easing the Passage* cannot help a reader choose when to die, but it does provide the information on measures that will permit a person to die tranquilly.

There are a number of obstacles to a tranquil death, some active, some matters of inertia. It is imperative for a reader to understand these obstacles so that the steps to overcome them are taken aggressively.

OBSTACLE ONE:
Ignorance

Few people are aware of the existing options in health care for the terminally ill. They do not know what to ask for or even whom to ask. This is true for the dying but competent patient, and it may be even more true for relatives who are informed—sometimes by long-distance telephone calls—that someone is dying or has had a crippling stroke. Ignorance of medical jargon, alternatives, and the law compounds the problem.

The first case that received widespread coverage in the media on the issue of easing the passage was that of Karen Ann Quinlan in 1976.

THE STORY OF KAREN ANN QUINLAN

The case of Karen Ann Quinlan attracted national attention and, until the Supreme Court decision on the Nancy Cruzan case, had the greatest impact on understanding the importance of advance written medical directives. In fact, it was the story of Karen Quinlan that sparked the very existence of Living Wills.

Karen Quinlan was admitted to the hospital in an unconscious state on April 15, 1975. Before admission she had stopped breathing for two fifteen-minute periods. At the hospital she was resuscitated and placed on a respirator. After testing, her physicians advised that they thought she would never regain consciousness and would persist in a vegetative state. But because she did not meet the criteria of brain death as defined by the Harvard Ad Hoc Committee, they refused to disconnect her respirator. Her father then asked the court to appoint him guardian with the right to order the withdrawal.

The Superior Court denied this authorization. Mr. Quinlan then appealed to the New Jersey Supreme Court. That court affirmed that Karen Ann Quinlan had the constitutional right to privacy and that her father, under the principle of substituted judgment, could make the decision to withdraw support. Most important, the court ruled that if death resulted from a withdrawal of ventilation support, it would be due to the cessation of extraordinary treatment and that a resulting death would be of natural causes. The respirator was removed, but Karen Quinlan did not die. When her physicians suggested that artificial feeding and hydration also be with-drawn, her father objected. (The Cruzan decision has elimi-nated any qualitative distinction between these therapies.) Karen Quinlan eventually died on June 11, 1985.

The Quinlan decision is important because it is the first time that the issue of withdrawing ventilating equipment from a permanently unconscious individual who was not brain-dead by the Harvard criteria was decided. The court also recognized that the issue at hand was not a new one and that it was constantly being resolved by physicians, patients, and their families. Only because there was disagreement between the parties, according to the court, was there need for it to reach judicial review.

There is a wider knowledge about easing the passage than there was two decades ago, yet surveys have indicated that most of the remedies and rights presented in this book are still known by only a small percentage of the population.

OBSTACLE TWO:
Inappropriate Medical Intervention

A passage from the President's Commission's report *Deciding to Forego Life-sustaining Treatment* (this report is discussed more fully in chapter 6) reads: "Biomedical developments of the past several decades have made death more a matter of deliberate decision. For almost any life-threatening condition, some intervention can now delay the moment of death. . . . [Events] once the province of fate have become a problem of human choice, a development that has profound ethical and legal implications."

We live in a culture with a can-do mentality: if it breaks, fix it. Tough week? Have some fun. Jimmy's little dog is run over. Mommy's response: "Don't cry, Jimmy. We'll get another." With our problem-solving abilities we can even "fix" death for a while. It is an evolution of the essential purpose of medicine: to cure. In the last twenty-five years dramatic breakthroughs have been made in "fixing" death. Although it cannot be prevented in the end, death can often be reversed: "dead" people can be brought back to life. Whether this is prolonging life or prolonging death and the degree to which "artificial life" is equivalent to human life are troubling issues.

The magic of reviving someone whose heart and lungs have ceased to operate is accomplished by cardiopulmonary resuscitation (CPR). When a person's heart and breathing have stopped, heretofore a definition of death, CPR can bring a person back from death. Although there were primitive ways in which resuscitation was attempted in earlier days (whipping a person with stinging nettles or blowing air down the throat with fireplace bellows), present-day CPR has existed for less than three decades. It is now standard practice. Partly because of the controlled circumstance and partly because of nervousness over legal consequences for not doing everything possible to keep a patient alive, CPR is routinely performed in hospitals. It is *policy* to perform CPR in all cases of cardiac arrest unless a physician's written directive specifying the contrary has been entered in the records. There are times when this is not only a lifesaving but a provident ability. For example, an otherwise healthy person undergoes surgery. While still under anesthesia, the heart stops as a result of unanticipated complications. Instant CPR administration restarts it. The patient recovers from surgery and is released back into normal life.

Easing the Passage is about the dying process, however, and in this context CPR can be characterized in many instances as prolonging *death*.

THE STORY OF MISS SEXTON

Miss Sexton is a ninety-seven-year-old woman who has suffered and recovered naturally from three heart attacks and a stroke. Substantial permanent damage has been done to

her heart muscle and part of her brain, however. She returns home from her latest hospitalization with chronic congestive heart failure, breathing difficulties, a partially
paralyzed right arm, and extreme weakness. The stroke has
also affected her ability to swallow easily, and she has lost
interest in eating. She is happy to be at home and hopes to
die there—in her sleep. Although medicine might not define
it thus, she is in the twilight of her life. Her body knows
this, as does her mind. Three weeks later she suffers a massive cardiac arrest. The person who is caring for her dials
911. By the time the ambulance arrives Miss Sexton has
been dead (that is, no palpable pulse or perceptible cardiac
output) for about eight minutes. The ambulance team immediately initiates CPR. The electrocardiograph (EKG)
monitor in the field reveals a disorganized electrical heart
activity called ventricular fibrillation, so the team shocks
her heart back to a regular rhythm with a defibrillator. Because she still had no spontaneous respirations (breathing
activity), she is ventilated by a mask and bag en route to the
hospital.

On Miss Sexton's arrival at the emergency department, an
endotracheal tube is inserted down her throat and the tube is
hooked up to a respirator. Lidocaine is administered contin-
uously through an intravenous line to maintain her heart
rhythm. The eight-minute lack of oxygen, however, has permanently damaged her brain. She has periods of apparent
consciousness, but other than being able to respond occasion-
ally to questions by a slight pressure with her fingers, she is
unable to express herself. She will have to be nourished by
tube and her lungs kept operative by the respirator. She may
live in this state for six days, six weeks, or six months. She
will never recover. Eventually, because medicine cannot prevent it forever, she will die of end-stage heart failure. Miss
Sexton's case is similar to that of Nancy Cruzan, except that
because of her medical history CPR probably should not have
been initiated.

Out-of-hospital CPR did not ease the passage in Miss Sexton's case, it obstructed it. It is, however, the norm today. Although CPR in the controlled situation of an operating room may have a high success record, a study published in the *Annals of Internal Medicine* revealed that this kind of ad hoc resuscitation, while often effective in bringing someone back to life, does not bring them back to health. The study considered 503 persons aged seventy years or older who received CPR. One hundred twelve (22 percent) survived initially; nineteen (4 percent) were discharged from the hospital. Of them, only eight were able to go home. The remaining eleven had to be institutionalized: two were severely debilitated, one was in a vegetative state, and two were severely demented. The study's principal author, Dr. Donald Murphy, commented, "How can we so willingly resuscitate an 80-year-old woman who's trying to die at home when the vast majority of health-care providers who are aware of the implications of CPR would refuse that treatment for themselves?"

The answer to that largely rhetorical question is that CPR is unique among medical procedures in that it is initiated *without a physician's order*. In fact, a specific order is required if CPR is *not* to be undertaken. An editorial in the *Annals* on the subject of the study stated: "In view of the findings of this study, it is perhaps time to establish meaningful guidelines for do-not-resuscitate orders in the elderly hospitalized patient in order to spare them costly, artificial, and uncomfortable measures that only serve to delay death." It is a salutary position but until now one that has not been acted on. Dr. Kathleen Nolan responded to the study's results: "CPR . . . should be less frequently used because patients have assumed more of a role in their own care. What I would like to see is for people to have more control of all medical interventions at the time of death." What is not indicated by these comments is that patients *do* have control, but they are unaware that they have it and do not know how to use it. It is this ignorance that *Easing the Passage* is intended to eliminate.

20

CPR has become an overused procedure, almost a knee-jerk reaction to cardiac arrest. In a single recent year, 1988, alone, the American Red Cross certified 2.5 million Americans to perform CPR. Combine this with the fact that successful outcome is rare if the person has chronic health problems and the potential for tragedy is enormous, as strangers on the street try their hand at bringing someone back to life. (Only two of the 244 patients in the *Annals* study who had out-of-hospital CPR left the hospital alive.) Analyzing this problem, the *Los Angeles Times* wrote: "Paramedics and emergency room doctors know from experience as well as research that, for an elderly patient from a nursing home, revival by CPR will most probably doom the patient to days or weeks in an intensive care unit, after which he will die anyway. Yet half of the in-hospital CPR attempts in this country are performed on people over 65."

A secondary consideration not often part of the decision-making process is that CPR on an elderly person means dealing with fragile bones. Some ribs are likely to be broken and, if the patient recovers, the outlook for any decent quality of life is minimal. The National Conference on Cardiopulmonary Resuscitation and Emergency Care concluded that "the purpose of CPR is the prevention of sudden, unexpected death. CPR is not indicated in certain situations, such as in the cases of terminal irreversible illness where death is not unexpected. . . . It has been suggested that *resuscitation in some circumstances may present a positive violation of a person's right to die with dignity*" (emphasis added).

There is a well-known cliché of mountaineers who are asked why they struggle to climb a perilous peak: because it is there. There is an analogy with CPR: the technique is there. Everybody dies of cardiopulmonary arrest. Everybody in the world dies that way. It is the ultimate cause of death cited on every death certificate. Thus every single dying person offers an opportunity for CPR; everyone is a candidate. The Brookings Institution recently published a book that argued that the authorization for CPR of critically ill patients should be turned around. Instead of requiring a written order *not* to resuscitate, the authors argue that CPR should be attempted only with positive consent.

CPR is not the only intervention in the dying process that can be an obstacle to easing the passage. There are so many artificial means of sustaining life that a person who once would have died in his sleep at home now lives on in an institution. The hospital intensive care unit (ICU), with its variety of monitors attached to a body, can prolong the dying process for a considerable period of time. The four physicians who compiled the Brookings study wrote that the ICU has become "an expensive, and often agonizing, preliminary to death—a rite of passage notable more for its rituals than for its rationality. The futility of many of these interventions can be predicted [for] patients who could be cared for more appropriately in less distressing settings." Some of these medical interventions are called "aggressive" or "heroic." It is also accurate to characterize them as bodily invasion, even assault and battery.

It is hoped that the disciplines of law, ethics, and medicine will one day revise procedures and policies to better align them with humanistic values. As the Brookings authors argued, these disciplines redefined death and brain death in the 1960s, and death-prolonging protocols should now be changed in a similar way. Until these protocols are changed, individuals must rely on the recourse spelled out in subsequent chapters.

OBSTACLE THREE:
The Legacy of Hippocrates

Hippocrates is considered the father of modern medicine, yet he died in the fourth century B.C., almost twenty-four-hundred years ago! His most enduring legacy is the Hippocratic Oath, which is sworn to by physicians. A basic anachronism is at work here. Physicians in the modern age of medical technology are potentially limited by a value judgment of a man who knew nothing of twentieth-century medical powers *and their effects*. Because of this irony, the Hippocratic Oath contributes to the ethical imbroglio over the obligation of a physician to keep a person alive at any cost. The Hippocratic Oath reads as follows:

> I swear by Apollo the physician, by Asclepius, Hygeia, and Panacea, and I take to witness all the gods, all the goddesses, to keep according to my ability and my judgment the following Oath:
>
> To consider dear to me as my parents him who taught me this art; to live in common with him and if necessary to share my goods with him; to look upon his children as my own brothers, to teach them this art if they so desire without fee or written promise; to impart to my sons and the sons of the master who taught me and the disciples who have enrolled themselves and have agreed to the rules of the profession, but to these alone, the precepts and the instruction. I will prescribe regimen for the good of my patients according to my ability and my judgment and never do harm to anyone. To please no one will I prescribe a deadly drug, nor give advice which may cause his death. Nor will I give a woman a pessary to procure abortion. But I will preserve the purity of my life and my art. I will not cut for stone, even for patients in whom the disease is manifest; I will leave this operation to be performed by practitioners (specialists in this art). In every house where I come I will enter only for the good of my patients, keeping myself far from all intentional ill-doing and all seduction, and especially from the pleasures of love with women or with men, be they free or slaves. All that may come to my knowledge in the exercise of my profession or outside of my profession or in daily commerce with men, which ought not to be spread abroad, I will keep secret and will never reveal. If I keep this oath faithfully, may I enjoy my life and practice my art, respected by all men and in all times; but if I swerve from it or violate it, may the reverse be my lot.

Remembering that the Hippocratic Oath is the only code of practice sworn to by physicians, the equivalent of the Pledge of Allegiance or the Presidential Oath of Office, it is useful to examine it a little further.

Why are practitioners of medicine, after four years of post-graduate training, at the end of the twentieth century, making oaths to some characters of Greek mythology? Why are they further taking as witness other gods and goddesses? Which ones are they thinking of as they hook up the dialysis machine? The oath is often given as the reason a physician can or cannot do something for a patient. But if the oath is sacrosanct, what of its promise that medical training will be without charge? That part is ignored. Some physicians are also known to have sex with patients (although in this day probably not slaves), another violation of the oath. Although foreswearing the seduction of patients and the doing of harm is laudatory, on the whole the Hippocratic Oath is archaic and has little application to modern medicine, of which its pagan author knew nothing.

The Hippocratic Oath is an obstacle to easing the passage: "To please no one will I . . . give advice which may cause his death." This appears to prohibit even the withdrawal of an artificial life-support system. Read in context, however, it can have a different interpretation. In his oath, Hippocrates took pains to distance himself from "ill-doing" to please someone "in every house where I come" other than a patient. In other words Hippocrates was vowing not to participate in the commission of a crime. In the oath this language can be used as an argument *for* easing the passage, even if it may shorten life: "I will prescribe regimen for the good of my patients according to my ability and my judgment."

This principle of beneficence is a well-established medical, legal, and ethical concept. Yet maintaining life at all costs is not always beneficent and, to the contrary, can be painful. Veterinarians complete medical training as rigorous as what a physician undergoes. They do not swear to the Hippocratic Oath and are free to release a sick and pained animal from its

24

misery, something they can accomplish by injection in less that fifteen seconds. Of course, there are religious, moral, ethical, and legal differences in the case of humans, but the final goal in the treatment of animals is the same as the desire of humans—a tranquil death. The Hippocratic Oath thus persists as a perceived obstacle to easing the passage.

Medicine, broadly defined, is composed of three elements:

- *Diagnosis:* What is wrong with you
- *Prognosis:* The likely outcome of your ailment
- *Therapy:* What a physician can do to change the natural course of your ailment

Hippocrates was a good diagnostician and an excellent prognostician: this is the problem, and this will be the outcome. In lieu of therapy, which barely existed in his day, arriving at an accurate diagnosis and prognosis was the best a physician could do, and he was seen as a soothsayer.

An ethical dilemma occurs today because there is an arsenal of therapies but not enough thought is going into their risks and benefits. The principle of beneficence, *primum non nocere* ("first, do no harm," from the Latin rendering of the oath), is entangled with its interpretation: do everything to maintain life.

"Hospital personnel and procedures are focused on keeping people alive. To permit a death which could have been postponed may seem a failure, a violation of regulations, or unethical. Intensive care begun under pressure of an emergency becomes difficult for family and physician to discontinue. Under these circumstances, a patient who wishes to refuse treatment is too often regarded as unruly and is restrained or drugged to make him or her more tractable." This comment by Ernest Morgan in his book *A Manual of Death Education* goes beyond the specifics of the Hippocratic Oath but involves it implicitly as a potential obstacle to easing the passage.

Physicians' Inability to Deal with Death

"Most physicians are not trained to provide terminal care."
That statement appeared in the august *Journal of the American Medical Association.* "Training in caring for the terminally ill should be part of all medical and nursing school curricula, and advanced training should be more widely available.... Improved prognostication in terminal illness, appropriate targeting of therapies, and improved pain and symptom control is essential," the article concluded.

Medical training both in school and residency programs hardly touches on terminal care. A good death, which could be considered the ultimate success, is not seen that way by most physicians, who view their role as stamping out disease. When the disease wins, they have lost. It is a conditioned position but not a good one. Because the field of medicine has become so highly specialized, the family physician who once helped a person through all illnesses, including sitting by the deathbed, is hard to find. Much more typical is a hospital scenario in which the terminally ill patient is referred to a series of specialists. In this situation, although the *medical* care may be state of the art, a more personal caring for easing the passage may be absent. It is a case of caring for an organism rather than a person, and physicians are quite skilled in keeping patients alive—even terminally ill ones.

Like other physicians, I (Hersh) spent four years in medical school. UCLA is considered a top medical institution, yet in those four years—well over five thousand hours of study— approximately *four* were involved in thanatology, a term used by one of my lecturers, Edwin Schneidman, for the psychosocial issues of death. It was considered a freshman "fluff" course as compared with biochemistry or anatomy. Obviously, these few hours could be only an overview. Death just was not part of the curriculum. Physicians are not formally trained in telling patients that they are going to die, let alone in easing the passage.

A physician learns about death while on the job. As an intern on duty he or she is responsible for a patient who cannot be roused. The patient has no auscultated heartbeat, no palpable pulse, no spontaneous respiration; the pupils are dilated and fixed in position, unable to constrict when exposed to bright light. An examination of the small veins in the back of the eyes with an ophthalmoscope reveals no pulsation. Death is pronounced at that moment. The intern has just encountered death but perhaps not dying.

I was fortunate. Because of a residency in family practice, I actually dealt with counseling and the psychological aspects of death. Family practitioners have a more psychosocial orientation than physicians in other specialties. Each year of my three-year residency I had a month-long rotation that focused on developing various kinds of counseling skills. Those of us in family practice were considered wimps, however, because we spent time on family dynamics, role playing, and so forth. Surgeons, internists, and the like did not have any similar training.

The difficulty in changing this deficiency in knowledge about terminal illness is that what a physician learns during training comes from the senior resident, who learned from his or her senior resident, so that medical training is like a big DNA of medicine. It only reproduces its own kind, and anyone who balks at the replication is suspect. In terms of humanism, to teach at what point you do *not* initiate another procedure, change must be engineered and mandated from the top and filtered down. Permitting a person to die with tranquility is contrary to the medical school norm, where everyone is looking for the "great case," and the patient becomes what in the jargon is "a flog" (as in flogging a dead horse), meaning some-

27

one who has no hope of a positive outcome but is put through many procedures. One may be horrified to read this and may rightly ask, "Can subjecting a patient to procedures that have no chance of success really be part of medical practice?" The answer is yes. In the most precise definition of the word *practice*, it *is* practice: a good deal of practice goes on before someone dies; procedures are attempted that the physician recognizes as hopeless.

Stating this will likely infuriate the medical community officially, but everyone who has been through medical training knows it is a fact. Any criticism of this statement will not be a refutation of the fact but a complaint that it has been aired. It needs to be aired for reasons that have to do with easing the passage. Such practice is one of several flaws in medical training that have been made public. For example, because of media coverage of two in-hospital deaths after admission for routine procedures, New York now has restrictions on the number of hours physicians-in-training can work. Investigations showed that the deaths were due to exhaustion-induced incompetence on the part of the treating physicians.

Why does a person decide to go into medicine? One reason may be to deal with a personal phobia of death: learning how to control disease. It is a fallacy, of course, that learning about disease allows a physician to master it; it only provides a *sense* of some control of one's own mortality. For physicians and patients alike, death will *always* win in the end. Confrontation with death is difficult for anyone, and physicians, like other people, have a resistance to acknowledging and dealing with death. There is the denial of their own deaths perhaps, as well as inexperience in dealing with death among patients. What is the most difficult undertaking physicians face? It is telling a person he or she is going to die. It is personally difficult. It is medically difficult as well, because physicians are unwilling to accept the fact that the person is dying: they want to try one more test, one more treatment. They cannot admit that they are themselves mortal and that they are confronted with a situation for which there is no magic bullet. So they continue to shoot one more time, reach into their clinical gun belt for something that is not there. They may do this even when treatment means more pain and suffering.

Speaking of the sometime reluctance of physicians to make a referral to Hospice, Ira Bates, vice president of the National Hospice Organization, said, "For that dying patient already in pain, it comes to the point where you have to say 'what are you doing?' It needs to be confronted by the medical community and physicians need to be educated in the issue of dying and death." Even the discussion of a patient's wishes for future care in case of emergency is avoided. "I'd rather shoot myself in the foot than start a Living Will discussion," said one physician. This presents a problem: Mrs. Smith, a reader of this book, wants to discuss advance medical directives with her physician. He has experience in death because patients die, but he does not have experience in dealing with the questions she wants to raise. It is important that she persevere, however (and the later chapters in this book will equip a reader with the knowledge to accomplish this). It also may help physicians to become open to the subject.

The reticence of physicians to discuss death and to develop a mind-set for easing the passage is an obstacle that should be addressed by the entire field of medicine. The possibility of mandatory training in thanatology is an appropriate consideration. The subject of death could be part of the required training for all medical students, or at least for those who go into specialties that involve interacting with dying patients.

———

I (Hersh) think I have a good approach to the subject, but it was gained ad hoc through experience and sharpened by the writing of this book. It is pointless for each physician to have to reinvent the wheel, because there are basic principles of dealing with death and dying issues.

The following true story written by Max Ferber, a Los Angeles businessman, was originally published in the *Los Angeles Times* and condensed in *Reader's Digest* in April 1976. It is an eloquent plea for a better education of medical professionals in helping the dying patient make a tranquil passage.

I cried, but not for Irma

It was six months ago that Irma and I first drove to the hospital. The internist had been concerned about my wife's occasional spotting. The gynecologist, apprehensive about what his examination indicated, had suggested a hysterectomy.

Following the operation, the surgeon came up to me in the waiting room. After some preliminary words he said: "It's terminal cancer."

It's terminal cancer.

In something of a whisper, I asked, "How long does she have?"

"It's difficult to say. It could be six months to five years."

Now Irma is dead, after six months, at 75.

It was not over her death that I cried. It was for the ignominious way of her going: the degradation of the spirit that was once her, the flagellation of her body, the torture inflicted by medical ethics and by a society that values the flesh over the spirit.

Irma recovered from the operation. She came home after three weeks in the hospital. During her convalescence she was up and about. She was at the table for meals. We visited friends, attended the theater, dined out. The pills were effective: there was no pain.

Had there been a remission? Were the doctors only mortals who had guessed wrong? Were we witnessing a miracle?

Two months of hope, then began the journey to the other shore. Irma was tired. Tempting her to eat was futile. Sedation was needed on a regular schedule. In the vigils through the night, we reacted to a gesture, kept adjusting her pillow. . . .

In time, the burden of caring became too great, even with family members sharing the shifts. Exhaustion set in—physical, mental, emotional. The only alternative was the hospital. "There are to be no heroic measures," I said. "I just don't want her to have any pain."

They said that they understood, but it was not to be.

The first ten days in the hospital were a time for gratitude. The nurses were kind and compassionate. Medication was given as needed. Irma's position was changed on schedule to prevent bed sores and to provide comfort. A tube hung from a bedside stand for intravenous feeding.

Irma was not aware of the world—but she was comfortable. There was no pain.

Each day, I watched, wondered—dulled to what was taking place but grateful to the nurses for their concern.

One morning of the third week, I entered the room and was startled. The intravenous tube had been removed from Irma's arm. Instead, she was being fed through a tube inserted in her nose.

She lay on her back in the bed, her hands tied to the rails. I asked why this had to be. "Because," the nurse said, "she was pulling out the tube."

Everyone was considerate. The nurses changed her position every two hours, retying her hands to the rails. They provided pillows to support her changed position. I saw her that evening on her side, tied down for immobility. Only her fingers twitched.

That night, at home in bed, I tried the various positions I had observed Irma take. I could hold each position for only fifteen minutes, having to shift to relieve the tension, to release the straining of my muscles. *But it was all right. Irma's position was being changed every two hours. She had no pain.* In the fifth week, a catheter was introduced to catch her urine. Now the chemicals that dripped through the tube inserted in her nose passed through her body and emptied efficiently into a pouch at the foot of her bed. In this way Irma was being kept alive. I paled at the sight.

The sixth week showed a change. Irma looked better: there was a flush in her cheeks; I wondered what this could mean.

"We pulled her through pneumonia by suctioning the mucus from her lungs," they said. "She is resting more easily now."

How thoughtful. The idea came to me: *Irma will make a good-looking corpse, thanks to medical science.* Through it all I was led to believe—by comments, by shrugging shoulders—

that it would be a matter of only two weeks. Always two weeks, by increments. At the end of three months, I was told Irma could no longer be kept in the hospital: she would have to be moved to a sanitarium.

That night I went to look over the sanitarium they had chosen. I was disheartened. The place was dim; it seemed gloomy and desolate.

The next morning, as usual, I stopped at the hospital. Irma's room was empty. She had been moved to the sanitarium earlier than I had expected. I hurried there. In daylight it looked better than it had by night.

I found the room where Irma was imprisoned. Yes, that word was inescapable. She was receiving the same care and attention as in the hospital. Again the tube was inserted in her nose, again the catheter pouch hung at the foot of her bed, again her hands were tied to the bed rails.

Irma's squirming had caused her sheet to slip off, and she was lying nude. . . .

Another six weeks passed.

Then at last, I was privileged to watch Irma being ferried across the River Styx. It had been a long journey, not because the river was wide—from where I stood, I had long since seen the opposite shrouded shore—but because the man-made current was almost irresistible. The force of public opinion, of medical and legal ethics, had run furiously, almost vengefully, resisting Irma's passage.

As I sat, patiently watching, I saw her finally reach the other shore and disappear into the mist of infinity. Her trials were over. It was Saturday, exactly 11:17 A.M. Society had claimed its last ounce of flesh, and after a while I could stop crying.

I left the sanitarium. As I drove away, a seething anger swept over me. It was a fetish, nothing less, for society to worship the flesh while it destroyed the spirit.

At any hospital, the dedication is heedlessly to prolong life. No, not just to prolong life but to do so by using ingenious devices that not only measure the semblance of life but also confirm that the machinery itself is functioning. . . .

The anger has not left me. It will consume me for as long as I live. Why are those who value living so insensitive to dying? In memory of Irma—for all the Irmas of this world—I make a simple but heartfelt plea: let us rise, all of us, to defend the defenseless body against the machine.

Definition of the Primary Organ

How do you determine that someone is dead? As recently as the nineteenth century, proof of death was partial decomposition of the body. The common proof in our age, clichéd in the movies, is to place an ear on the person's chest and listen for a heartbeat, to feel for a pulse, and to hold a mirror to the nose or mouth to check for fog indicating breathing. If these signs are absent, the person is dead. That system *used* to work and was essentially what a physician said in medical terms: no spontaneous respiration, no auscultated heartbeat.

But no longer.

At issue: what is the primary organ? Most think of the heart. Medicine and law have changed this, however. The primary organ is the brain. This definition has been the basis of a number of court cases that wrestle with the issue of when it is appropriate to withhold or withdraw artificial treatments that are extending life.

The need to change the definition of death has a curious and even macabre origin: the development of organ transplantation technology. The locus of life and death was shifted from the heart and lungs to the brain so that a person could be called dead while still having a beating heart and spontaneous or induced respiration. This change was brought about by the need to "harvest" organs (the medical phrase). What have become known as the "Harvard criteria" redefined death according to a measurement of electrical activity in the brain. With this new definition it became possible to declare someone dead before the heart and lungs had stopped delivering blood; consequently these organs were alive and healthy for transplantation purposes. The Harvard criteria have only limited application to the subject of easing the passage, because, by definition, someone who meets those standards is already dead even if his or her heart is beating. Medically it is a "clean case," similar to that of the competent person who says, "I do not want that treatment." In both instances the physician does not treat; in the former case because physicians do not treat dead people, in the latter because it is the patient's right to refuse treatment. *Easing the Passage* is concerned with all those people in between who may not represent clean cases to a physician.

There is, however, a strange irony in this matter of definitions. A person whose heart is beating may be legally defined as dead, whereas a person whose heart has stopped is not necessarily considered dead, and a physician may risk a lawsuit if he or she does not attempt to resuscitate.

The brain, like the heart, is made of nonregenerative tissue. That is to say that damaged, inert tissue is not replaced by new, living matter. The brain is an organ of several major parts. One part of the brain controls conscious thought and the facets of intelligence that contribute to personality. A person may suffer permanent brain damage (as in Nancy Cruzan's case) leaving him or her in an incurable vegetative state. Yet a primitive part of the brain, called the brain stem, sends signals that regulate the heart and lungs. To be kept alive in this condition, however, a person must be fed artificially. In other coma cases the person can be kept alive only by mechanical breathing in addition to artificial feeding. Thus the definition of death as a measurement of brain function keeps people alive who formerly would have died.

OBSTACLE SIX:
The 4 Percent Reality

A recent study showed that only 4 percent of the hospitals in the United States ask patients on admission if they have executed Living Wills. Admittedly, only a small number of the population have done so, but for the 12 percent that have, failure to determine the existence of this document is a denial of their rights. This almost blanket disregard of a legal document is shocking.

A practical form of protection against this abuse would be a computerized master list in the hospital that would be available to emergency departments and ambulance services. This could be instituted rather simply in the health care services of smaller communities, but it would be a problem in large urban situations with overlapping jurisdictions. Until standard procedures change, however, the admitting physician who determines that a patient has a Living Will is one of a tiny minority.

————

In my (Hersh's) hospital, we set up a task force to expand the community's understanding of Living Wills. Our first thought was to discuss it with everyone on admission as just one more question, but we decided it would give people the creeps. It was also uncomfortable for surgeons and anesthesiologists, who believed it might lead to a sense of lost confidence. Another idea was to do it on patient discharge, but again individual physicians might have objected. Our tentative plan is to educate patients within the hospital mostly through the nursing staff who, as counselors, could explain the Living Will form. We are also planning a massive outreach to the community in which we discuss advance medical directives and provide forms (and witnesses) for people to take advantage of right then or to take to their attorneys to review and execute. Because it is done as a hospital service, that information will then be filed on a patient's record and on a master list in the emergency department, with the local ambulance service, and, of course, with the individual's personal physician.

————

Another impediment to getting advance medical directives promoted by the medical community is that physicians are also businesspeople who believe they may jeopardize a continued client relationship if they advocate medical directives as precaution for the future. It was not the airlines—to cite a parallel situation—that came up with the passenger advice that is announced before every flight: "In the unlikely event of a water landing, your seat cushion can be used as a flotation device." It was the Federal Aviation Administration, which regulates the airlines, that made this announcement a requirement, but the subtle phrasing was probably influenced by the airline companies. "A water landing," for example, is a crash, and the very mention of a "flotation device" is a subtle reassurance that one will survive the crash, be able to exit the plane before it sinks or explodes, and float safely until a rescue vessel arrives.

A Living Will does not contain euphemisms, and a surgeon about to perform a gallbladder operation might not consider it therapeutic to inquire about a Living Will. Such an inquiry could undermine the patient's confidence of the surgeon's abilities.

OBSTACLE SEVEN:

Procrastination

"Death is un-American" wrote Arnold Toynbee. We have been brought up with such a sense of the invincibility of our country, democracy, and way of life that we lump in death as another failure we need not consider. Even with an acknowledgment of our mortality, the phantasmagoria of the generation gap infects our thinking.

Carter Woodward is fifty and has two grown children of twenty-seven and twenty-three. His wife is fifty-one, his mother is eighty. The latter has clipped a news story about Living Wills from a newspaper, and has asked her son about it. He plans to help her get a form to execute when he sees her at Thanksgiving.

Five potential tragedies are contained in this true scenario. With no advance directives regarding medical wishes, a wife, a mother, two children, and Woodward himself are being left vulnerable to an accident. Recalling again Nancy Cruzan's case, the state of Missouri, for many years, would not allow Cruzan to die because she never formally indicated while mentally competent in a legally acceptable way that she did not wish to live in a persistent vegetative state by means of artificial feeding. Why should the healthy young members of the Woodward family execute a Living Will *now?* That's why.

The General Counsel of the American Medical Association has made this case to its membership, urging physicians to bring the subject of advance health directives to the attention of their patients.

> While it is often difficult for people to discuss their own death in a concrete way, it is becoming increasingly important for individuals to express their preferences regarding the use of artificial life supports. For perhaps *70 percent* [emphasis added] of Americans, a decision will be made by others whether to provide life-sustaining medical care when devastating illness becomes terminal or irreversible. Making these decisions in advance will ensure not only that the patient's wishes are carried out but also that family members and friends can act on the patient's behalf with the confidence that they are acting in the patient's best interests.

OBSTACLE EIGHT:
The Law

Although a considerable body of legislated and case law *supports* easing the passage, individual states have passed different laws about what is permissible in acts and omissions that could ease the passage. Because of these ambiguities, physicians and hospitals are sensitive to both liability for civil malpractice and possible criminal prosecution.

The Constitution affirms the right to privacy, but it says nothing about any right to die. Like the Hippocratic Oath, the Constitution was written before it was known that medicine could pull a person back from death. Lawyers and judges who read the Constitution narrowly note the omission. Because the Founding Fathers were a group of rugged individualists, however, had they foreseen this legal impediment, it is likely they would have extended the right to privacy to the specific right to refuse death-prolonging procedures.

One of the principal controversies in the laws governing easing the passage is whether artificial administration of nutrition and hydration is subject to withholding and withdrawal. The argument that it is *not* permissible to refuse such things is made on the premise that the taking of food and liquids is not a medical treatment but a natural process, and therefore is not subject to withdrawing or withholding. The Connecticut Supreme Court, however, recently observed that artificial feeding devices such as tubes inserted into the nose to feed the stomach were qualitatively different from "a spoon or a straw."

The argument that artificial administration of food and hydration *is* a medical procedure is further buttressed by the fact that these substances are regulated by the Food and Drug Administration. As an attorney for the organization Concern for the Dying wrote, "The nutrition formulas supplied through these tubes are listed in the *Physicians' Desk Reference*, making them a far cry from the recipes featured in the *Joy of Cooking*."

This issue has not been resolved with any uniformity, and certain states *exclude* the right to refuse artificial nutrition and hydration in their Living Will statutes.

THE STORY OF ESTELLE BROWNING

Estelle Browning was eighty-nine years old when she suffered a massive stroke that caused irreversible brain damage and left her incompetent. She had executed a Florida Living Will in which she had specifically stated that artificial feeding should not be given should she be in a terminal condition with no hope of recovery.

Browning's guardian asked the court for permission to withdraw the artificial feeding. The court denied the request. The decision was appealed, and the appellate court affirmed that Browning had a "constitutional right" to have the feeding discontinued and that her guardian could exercise this right without court permission.

The local district attorney, however, appealed that decision to the Florida Supreme Court, despite the appellate court's statement that Browning should not be "yet another citizen who received her constitutional right to privacy posthumously."

Estelle Browning died before her case was heard.

Compounding the injustice, the tragedy of Estelle Browning may also have been affected by sexism. A study reported in *Law, Medicine and Health Care* found that courts are less likely to honor a woman's wishes than a man's in matters of life-support systems. Reporting on the findings, the *New York Times* stated,

> In a study of 22 right-to-die decisions from appeals courts in 14 states, Dr. Steven Miles found that women are consistently portrayed as less capable of rational decision-making than men. . . . Women are referred to by their first names, and constructed as emotional, immature, unreflective, and vulnerable to medical neglect, while men are called by their last names, and constructed as rational, mature, decisive, and assaulted by medical technology.

A number of organizations, including the American Medical Association and the American Academy of Family Practice, are challenging the interpretation that artificial nutrition and hydration cannot be refused. The Alzheimer's Disease and Related Disorders Association has affirmed that

> it is ethically permissible for the physician to withhold treatment that would serve mainly to prolong the dying process . . .

when the severely demented patient has previously made his or her wishes known. . . . If such a patient rejects food and water by mouth, it is ethically permissible to withhold nutrition and hydration artificially administered by vein or gastric tube. Spoon feeding should be continued if needed for comfort.

Arguing as *amicus curiae* before the U.S. Supreme Court in the Cruzan case, the National Hospice Organization made the following argument:

Neither the state legislature nor the Missouri Supreme Court has explained why the State's concern with protecting life requires forcing substances into dying bodies through feeding tubes, while not requiring forcing oxygen into those bodies through ventilators. Yet the State permits the latter to be refused but not the former. Because there is no justification for this dissimilar treatment (i.e., between patients whose nourishment is provided mechanically and those whose respiration or kidney function are provided mechanically), the State's action in this case not only subverts fundamental constitutional liberties, it also violates the Equal Protection Clause of the Fourteenth Amendment.

Although the finding of the court went against the Cruzans' request to withdraw the artificial feeding of their daughter, the court did find that there is no difference between artificially administered nutrition and hydration and other artificial and mechanical life-sustaining measures.

Aside from questions of valid legal status of documents approved by law (discussed in the next chapter), such documents are not necessarily adhered to by physicians and hospitals. In the case of the simpler documents, they may be construed as too vague to dictate whether a particular treatment is or is not to be undertaken. In the case of the more specific documents, explicit instructions on a variety of medical options may not cover a procedure unknown at the time the document was executed.

OBSTACLE NINE:
Insurance

Willis Goldbeck, a former president of the Washington Business Group on Health, has cited a major problem in health care delivery in this country: "The United States rations care daily in both the public and private sectors. People do not have equal access to even the most basic services."

Insurance coverage for the terminally ill patient encompasses the triad of the good, the bad, and the ugly. Since 1983 Medicare has approved the coverage of certain Hospice care and a *limited* amount of home care. It reimburses nursing home expenses only in cases that require skilled nursing. This is the good news.

The bad part of health insurance policy, generally, is that it has been slow in broadening coverage to include a host of physician, equipment, and pharmaceutical needs of terminally ill patients who choose to die at home.

A change is not going to come until Medicare realizes that, just as it has opened up some home health care areas for reimbursement, it must reimburse physician costs. Insurance carriers need to respect that when a patient has a qualified medical problem an either/or situation exists. The physician can send the patient into the hospital and run up the bill, or he can handle the illness at home. Medicare needs to acknowledge that home care is appropriate and that a physician should be reimbursed at a proper rate, so that it becomes cost-effective for a physician to provide medical care in the home.

This is happening, but not as quickly as it should. The tendency has been that a person who needs long-term static antibiotic therapy, for example, is placed in a hospital to lie about for six or eight weeks only because of the intravenous capability. Another reason for hospitalization is that insurance sometimes covers the therapy only when it takes place in an inpatient facility. This is so contrary to the best interest of Medicare and private insurance companies that change is bound to come. Studies have shown that as much as 80 percent of a patient's *lifetime* medical expenses are incurred in the final weeks of life in futile, high-technology situations. More than $100,000 may be expended during this period, which is then paid by Medicare or a supplemental insurance carrier.

Another difficulty is raised by the insurance qualifications. For example, in the case of a stroke victim it is necessary to keep enough Medicare-approved treatments in place to qualify. If the intravenous tubing is withdrawn, the patient may lose the Medicare payment. Some hospitals absorb this expense, but others issue to the patient a formal letter of denial of service.

Medicaid patients have even more difficulty in the hospital. Hospitals must have a minimum number of Medicaid beds to qualify for a license, but they seldom have a single extra bed because the reimbursement is so marginal.

There is an uglier side to this. Hospitals are not necessarily the healthiest place to be, because the issue of financing, which may seem remote to patient autonomy, can get very intermingled with treatment. Medicare and Medicaid had a funding crisis a few years ago and are in the midst of another one. They dealt with the one at the beginning of the 1980s by creating diagnostically related groups (DRGs). (Medicare previously had a limit, and a supplemental insurance carrier or the patient could be asked to pay the difference between the bill and the Medicare limit.) Hospitals currently receive a specified amount per person per treated diagnosis (statement of the ailment), and physicians soon will. The estimated course of the illness (prognosis), any complications that may arise, and the therapy used to deal with the illness are not relevant.

A DRG has been computed for every ailment by setting a limited number of hospital days, multiplying it by a dollar value per day, and multiplying the product by a factor that accounts for geographical disparities. Thus if a patient is admitted with a particular diagnosis that allows for nine hospital days and either dies or is discharged in five days, the hospital keeps the difference. If the stay exceeds the formula, Medicare will cut off payment to the hospital for that service. Private insurance has no obligation to pay beyond the Medicare obligation.

In a Pavlovian way, the government, through Medicare, is going to train hospitals over time to limit care. This may benefit people who have complained about excessive treatment, so in terms of easing the passage it might turn out to be a good thing, but for all the wrong reasons. Social Darwinism is what one Princeton economist has tagged the growing survival of the insurance-fittest. Although treatment is not yet *widely* denied to the indigent, some hospitals do not accept any transfer or even admission without first clearing it with the hospital administration. This can be especially true of Medicare admissions. Thus nonmedical personnel—cost managers—are intruding in a process that is medical. This double standard between those who are well-covered and those who are not is not limited to terminal care but spills over into it. Late in 1990 the *Boston Globe* reported:

> New research is documenting how well-insured patients get access to the full panoply of technology while physicians offer uninsured or Medicaid patients strikingly less. . . . A Massachusetts study shows that heart patients with private insurance are much more likely to get a key diagnostic test, undergo by-pass surgery or have artery-clearing treatment than similar patients who are uninsured or depend on Medicaid. . . . Health researchers believe well-insured patients may get too much expensive and risky care, while those who lack coverage . . . are denied necessary and even life-saving care.

———

I (Hersh) sent an elderly Medicare patient to a hospital about thirty miles away because I wanted him under the care of a respiratory specialist there. He stabilized after treatment but was not ready to go home. Because the specialist could do nothing more, he called and asked if I would like the patient back at my own hospital where I could resume management of his health care. I said, "absolutely." Afterward, the administrator in my hospital read me the riot act because I had taken a "financial loser," and worse, I had taken a loser *already under someone else's roof, and most of the insurance allocation had been made to the other hospital.*

―――――

It is this formula of DRG reimbursement that has forced the closing of so many small community and private hospitals in this country, because it is not possible to quantify illness in this way. A bleeding ulcer, for example, might require forty-eight hours of hospitalization or three weeks. A large institution can get by on the averages of "winners" and "losers," but a twenty-bed hospital could be ruined by a case that was covered for a few days but turned out to require a few months of treatment.

People covered by a group health policy may also find that there is a financial disincentive for treatment, especially if the policy is written by a health maintenance organization (HMO). HMOs are companies that bring the risk down a level from the insurance company to the physician. The HMO takes the money it collects on a per-employee basis from a company and skims 10 to 15 percent of income off the amount, with no risk. The balance is available to physicians. The physician promises to provide comprehensive medical coverage for a fixed amount. It is a gamble and obviously has a societal implication, because the physician is now making money by *not doing things to an HMO patient.* Perhaps this is no worse than the ethics of making money by *doing* things—the unnecessary cardiogram just to load the bill. However, when it gets to "Shall I do an operation, or use a more economical treatment?" the potential for abuse is created. In the HMO scene a physician can make money by not initiating a procedure.

Currently, terminally ill patients receive life-sustaining procedures unless the patient or surrogate rejects it. This could change to a situation in which these procedures are *not* provided unless requested.

THE STORY OF CLARENCE HERBERT

Clarence Herbert was admitted to the hospital for routine surgery. During the operation, he went into cardiac arrest. He was resuscitated and hooked up to a respirator. After three days Herbert's physicians informed his family that he would not regain consciousness. At that point the family agreed to have the respirator removed. Herbert, however, continued to breathe without artificial assistance. After two days, again with family consent, his intravenous nutrition and hydration lines were removed. Herbert died shortly thereafter.

The two physicians were charged with murder and conspiracy to commit murder, but they never came to trial because the court dismissed the charges. The basis of the charge in this unusual criminal case was that because the physicians were being paid by an HMO, they stood to gain economically if there was no further need for treatment and so had prematurely decided to end Clarence Herbert's life.

OBSTACLE TEN:
Religious Faith

Although many religions affirm the sanctity of life, some care givers have stricter views that withholding or withdrawing artificial life-supporting equipment is akin to playing God, hence heretical behavior. This position ignores the fact that, as a Methodist clergyman put it, "We do not leave birth to God." It is likewise contrary to the view of the Vatican: refusing treatment "is not equivalent to suicide; on the contrary, it should be considered as an acceptance of the human condition."

THE STORY OF DR. ENGLISH

Dr. English had a family practice in a group of isolated New-foundland fishing communities. One of his patients was dying of a crippling and painful cancer. The man was very old, had been a proud and independent fisherman all his life, and was one of the physician's personal friends. "Please," he begged Dr. English, "let me die as I lived. Now. Before I am unable to deal with the pain and have to ask for help." Knowing that the man had only a few weeks of life remaining in any case, Dr. English asked the clinic's nurse to draw a syringe of morphine. The nurse, however, was a Pentecostal, and after stating that she insisted that God should determine when and how the man died, threatened to call in the police if the morphine was administered. So Dr. English, as he put it, "failed his old friend." As the disease ran its course he gave medication only when at last the fisherman could no longer take the pain and had to ask for it. Ten years after his friend's death, the physician still believes that the incident was his worst betrayal of his medical vows. "I was a coward, and because of it did not serve my patient."

(Had Dr. English given the dose of morphine, he would have been guilty of murder under current U.S. law.)

CHAPTER FIVE

Easing the Passage:
The Paperwork

Advance medical instructions, of which Living Wills are the most familiar, are a recent development in health care documents. By the late 1960s their need became evident, as the development of life-extending technologies—respirators, endotracheal tubes, dialysis machines, and artificial and invasive nutritional procedures such as nasogastric feeding, intravenous hydration, and hyperalimentation—meant that dying a natural death was no longer ensured.

This technical ability to extend the process of dying created a new hardship for many terminally ill people. Before the creation of Living Wills, it was difficult both for relatives to make decisions on a patient's behalf and for physicians not to take every measure to prolong a life. The Society for the Right to Die created the original prototype of a Living Will, which allowed a person to express specific directions for medical treatment during terminal illness, lifting the burden of decision from the shoulders of the family, physicians, and others. In the past decade this organization has distributed eight million Living Wills. During the same period a number of celebrated court cases have heightened public awareness of the excruciating dilemmas that can arise when a patient's wishes are not expressed in writing.

Yet today only a small minority of the U.S. adult population have executed Living Wills and other equally important related documents. Although some surveys have indicated that as many as 18 percent of the population have completed

47

some advance medical directive, this estimation is suspect. A survey conducted in Maine just before the Cruzan decision indicated that 75 percent of the state's population had never even *heard* of a Living Will and that only 5 to 6 percent had executed one. Another study quoted the national percentage as 9. Ignorance and procrastination, as discussed in chapter 4, are the major culprits in this delay, fueled by a sense of "It isn't going to happen to me, or at least not for a while." Since a person's right to informed consent has legal force, postponing execution of such a document while hoping for a tranquil death is only gambling against oneself.

The case of Nancy Cruzan is today's most visible example of the sorrows attendant on a failure to execute a Living Will. Nancy Cruzan was reported to have *said in conversations* with friends that she would not want to be kept alive by artificial means if there were no hope for her recovery. The state of Missouri, however, declared that these recollections by her family were "vague and unreliable": in the face of "the uncertainty of Nancy's wishes and her own right to life, we choose to err on the side of life, respecting the rights of incompetent persons who may wish to live despite a severely diminished quality of life."

A second factor for "clear and convincing evidence" that a comatose patient would not wish to continue living by artificial means was presented in a number of briefs before the U.S. Supreme Court in Nancy Cruzan's case. Families of comatose patients, it was argued, may have considerable financial interest in the outcome and hence could desire withdrawal of life-support systems for personal interest rather than the patient's best interest.

There is another reason for executing a Living Will or other medical directives. Too often, physicians turn to the family of a patient for advice *before* the patient is incompetent. Dr. Christine K. Cassel of the University of Chicago Pritzker School of Medicine stated: "We've been encouraged to move too quickly from the patient to the family, sometimes even

48

when the patient may still be able to clearly state his values. Just because a patient shows some deficits on a mental status exam doesn't mean he should automatically be considered incompetent." Advance care documents limit a family's decisions to the patient's previously expressed wishes.

The reader is reminded that the initiative in completing the paperwork falls on the individual, not the physician. This situation will improve with legislation, now law, that was introduced in Congress by Senators John C. Danforth of Missouri and Patrick Moynihan of New York. Known as the Patient Self-Determination Act, health care providers that receive funds from Medicare or Medicaid must now inform patients of the availability of advance care documents, e.g., Living Wills, and maintain written records of a patient's wishes in this regard and comply with such directions. Nonetheless physicians may still be reticent about bringing up these documents during a routine visit. "Oh my God, I'm here for a sore throat, and my doctor is asking me if I've written down my wishes for terminal care!" Initiating such a conversation may also bring into question the physician's competence: "If he's asking me to consider a Living Will, maybe he doesn't know how to cure my current ailment." Or perhaps, "The doctor isn't being truthful about my sore throat. Maybe something is seriously wrong." After placing a poster about Living Wills in the waiting room, some physicians find discussing advance medical instructions is not awkward anymore. Patients read the poster and ask about what is involved, and they often proceed to execute Living Wills.

What I (Hersh) have found is that people are rarely threatened, and are usually appreciative, when I tell them about Living Wills. (We have four rubber stamps in the office: two are for checks, one is for noting allergies, and one reads "Living Will on file.")

Readers should prepare advance medical instructions (as described in the following), informing their physicians and family members of their action, and distribute copies of the document.

Living Will

A Living Will is a document signed by an individual in a competent state that delineates his or her wishes for life-sustaining procedures should he or she no longer be able to express them.

A Living Will ranges from a simple four-sentence declaration to a more detailed advance statement of choices made among various medical options. Because Living Wills gain force by state legislation, no set language has been accepted by all the states. To the contrary, there is outright confusion and contradiction among the states. The American Jewish Congress, among other organizations, has argued for a more rational focus on the protection of an individual's rights and "public policies to enable individuals to create advance directives." It also pointed out that "some Living Will laws appear to limit patients' ability to refuse treatment by imposing excessive substantive restrictions or procedural requirements."

What follows is an example of the simplest form of a Living Will. Even for someone living in a state that has no Living Will legislation, executing such a form generally has force under case law. Furthermore, because states vary on the wording they require for Living Wills, it makes sense to execute this more general document as well as a specific state-approved one. Should someone have an accident that left them permanently unconscious while away from their home state, a Living Will executed according to their own state's language restrictions might not apply, whereas a more generally phrased document might.

Sample Living Will

To my family, doctors, and all those concerned with my care:

I, _____ , being of sound mind, make this statement as a directive to be followed if I become unable to participate in decisions regarding my medical care.

If I should be in an incurable or irreversible mental or physical condition with no reasonable expectation of recovery, I direct my attending physician to withhold or withdraw treatment that merely prolongs my dying. I further direct that treatment be limited to measures to keep me comfortable and to relieve pain.

These directions express my legal right to refuse treatment. Therefore, I expect my family, doctors, and everyone concerned with my care to regard themselves as legally and morally bound to act in accord with my wishes and, in so doing, to be free of any legal liability for having followed my directions.

_____
Signature

Such a general statement usually carries some weight but can be *very* open to interpretation. This can prevent a patient's true intent from being carried out if there is family or physician disagreement on interpretation. Family members may feel guilty or fear criticism if they forego treatment, and the physician may be concerned about liability. All Living Wills are a variant of the above language, but they differ from state to state in terms of specificity, witnesses, and so forth. And even states that have Living Will statutes change them. Maine provides an example of what this could mean to a resident. When the state enacted a Living Will law in 1985, it suggested a simple language:

If I should have an incurable or irreversible condition that will cause my death within a short time, and if I am unable to participate in decisions regarding my medical treatment, I direct my attending physician to withhold or withdraw procedures that merely prolong the dying.

51

Some fifty thousand residents of Maine signed such documents. In 1990, however, the Maine legislature enacted a new law requiring the document to contain more specific language and to designate an individual empowered to act on the signer's behalf if he or she were no longer able to communicate. The new law also added particular reference to the withholding or withdrawal of artificially administered nutrition and hydration. This new addition is welcome, in general. As discussed in chapter 4, one of the cloudy issues in the courts has been whether nutrition and fluids constitute treatment—and hence might be withheld—or whether they are natural processes that could not then be withheld. By allowing the signatory of a Living Will the opportunity to specifically direct the physician in this matter, a Maine resident could guarantee that dying would not be prolonged by artificially administered nutrition and hydration.

But all of the fifty thousand Maine residents who already signed a Living Will without this specific language are not likely to be aware of this new legislation. They did what was appropriate, took the prudent step of executing a Living Will—was that not enough?

Unfortunately, because the new act specifically isolates artificial nutrition and hydration, anyone with only the previous general language of a Living Will *cannot have artificial nutrition and hydration withheld or withdrawn* unless able to demand it verbally.

Some states mandate a renewal of a Living Will every five years. One organization suggests updating the signature every year. Because of public consciousness about Living Wills in particular and the whole issue of death with dignity in general, some states are moving quickly to create or upgrade legislation, including requirements for the qualifications of a witness (for example, not a relative). This trend is welcome, but it means that one should stay abreast of current law in the state in which they live.

Fortunately, there is one organization that does this for the residents of all fifty states. Two organizations—the Society for the Right to Die and Concern for Dying—are in the process of amalgamating into a single organization. This nonprofit group depends entirely on the support of individual contributors. Among other activities, the society maintains an up-to-date file on the prescribed language of Living Wills and other advance medical directives for each state. In addition to a newsletter on the subject, they provide their members with specific forms relative to the individual states of residency. Currently, their annual fee for membership is $15. Immediately after the Supreme Court's decision in the Cruzan case, the *New York Times* featured the organization on its editorial page. During the next three months, the society received more than 250,000 requests for Living Wills, and the volume continues; its staff has swelled to almost one hundred. The society has also created a program whereby corporations can arrange for their employees to receive the appropriate documents and updates.

Forty-two states (as well as the District of Columbia) now have Living Will legislation. They are:

Alabama	Kansas	Oklahoma
Alaska	Kentucky	Oregon
Arizona	Louisiana	South Carolina
Arkansas	Maine	South Dakota
California	Maryland	Tennessee
Colorado	Minnesota	Texas
Connecticut	Mississippi	Utah
Delaware	Missouri	Vermont
Florida	Montana	Virginia
Georgia	Nevada	Washington
Hawaii	New Hampshire	West Virginia
Idaho	New Mexico	Wisconsin
Illinois	North Carolina	Wyoming
Indiana	North Dakota	District of Columbia
Iowa		

Legislation is pending in Massachusetts, Michigan, Nebraska, New Jersey, New York, Ohio, Pennsylvania, and Rhode Island.

By executing a Living Will a person goes a long way to avoid the kind of problem the Cruzan family faced: it specifies what care one wishes given and *not* given if in a terminal situation or (in some states) a persistent vegetative state with no hope of regaining consciousness. Combined with the constitutional and common law right to refuse treatment, a signed, properly witnessed Living Will provides protection from unwanted life-prolonging procedures that in fact prolong death.

A Living Will does not, however, flatly prohibit the saving of its signer from imminent death. During routine surgery, if an otherwise healthy patient suffers a cardiac arrest, the surgical team is likely to quickly restart the heart. This is one of the few times when CPR makes some sense. Routine surgery does not create a terminal condition, and there is nothing to indicate the patient's condition will be hopeless. A Living Will does not say that a healthy person cannot be rescued.

THE STORY OF GEORGE FIELD

George Field was working in the machine shop when he suddenly experienced crushing chest pain. He had been sweating in the exertion of work and heat, and his potassium was low. He was raced to the hospital by his boss. In the emergency department he was given nitroglycerin, and he recovered. He was placed in the cardiac unit. There he was chatting about his Living Will with an intern who was making his rounds when the latter glanced at the monitor. The pattern was flickering. Field was still awake and alert, but a fatal arrhythmia was showing on the screen. A quick injection of potassium and he was back from certain death with no damage.

Health Care Proxy

The Living Will is the document most familiar to most people, but two additional documents are equally important. Both are ways by which people can appoint someone to speak for them in medical matters if they themselves are no longer able to do so. One is a health care proxy; the other (described below) is a Durable Power of Attorney for Health Care. Health care proxies are normally designated in the language of a state's Living Will legislation and are part of the Living Will form itself. However, the advantage of the single document is outweighed by a limitation. Many Living Will statutes impose limitations on a health care proxy's validity, including application only when a patient's condition is terminal—not, for example, when the patient is in a permanent vegetative state. And *terminal* is variously described as imminent death, death within a few days, death within six months, and so on. The proxy, then, becomes limited by the same exclusions that govern the Living Will. Thus a person in an advanced state of Alzheimer's disease may not be able to express any wish, but because the disease is not terminal, he would not be able to have a proxy speak in his behalf, whereas someone with a Durable Power of Attorney for Health Care would.

The states that authorize proxy appointments through their Living Will acts are Arkansas, Delaware, Florida, Idaho, Indiana, Louisiana, Maine, Minnesota, Texas, Utah, Virginia, and Wyoming.

The following is a sample statement of proxy designation:

If I should have an incurable and irreversible condition that, without the administration of life-sustaining treatment, will, in the opinion of my attending physician, cause my death within a relatively short time, and I am no longer able to make or communicate decisions regarding my medical treatment, I appoint _____ or, if he or she is not reasonably available or is unwilling to serve, _____ , to make decisions on my behalf regarding withholding or withdrawal of such treatment that only prolongs the process of dying and is not necessary for my comfort or to alleviate pain, pursuant to the Uniform Rights of the Terminally Ill Act of this state.

_____
Signature

Durable Power of Attorney
for Health Care

A Durable Power of Attorney for Health Care is a legal document that appoints a guardian to make decisions on a patient's behalf should he become incompetent or unable to speak for himself. The guardian so named is expected to be familiar with the patient's wishes and to make decisions in accord with those wishes. A Durable Power of Attorney for Health Care normally has more authority than a proxy (and, in some cases, a Living Will).

A power of attorney is a common legal document that deputizes an agent to act in a person's behalf. It has the same limitations for the agent as for the principal. Thus if the principal becomes incompetent, the attorney is incompetent to act on the principal's behalf. To bypass this anomaly, every U. S. state has enacted laws that authorize a *durable* power of attorney. Under this document, an agent remains able to represent the principal even if the latter is incompetent. Not all states have enacted specific legislation covering Durable Powers of Attorney for *Health Care*. These documents normally are accepted by the court, however, even without specific state legislation. The Durable Power of Attorney for Health Care usually allows the agent to make decisions without initially seeking court approval.

A Durable Power of Attorney for Health Care is of parallel importance to a Living Will. There have been occasions in which someone has been in a terminal or persistently vegetative condition and the Living Will is either out of date or has not specified particular procedures. In the absence of legally acceptable advance declaration of wishes, states have argued that they are required to protect life, hence to use medical techniques that could have been excluded by written declaration. As already described, the Living Wills of some states cover only the terminal condition. Someone who is in a persistent vegetative state is not necessarily a terminal case within the meaning of the law and in fact might live for decades. A designated agent, however, normally is allowed to refuse treatment on behalf of the patient in such a circumstance. Another argument for the durable power is to allow decisions to be made at a future time when new medical knowledge may have evolved. For example, just before this book went to press, a study was published that claimed that continued artificial hydration for a terminal patient may cause additional *discomfort*. A designated agent could act on this information on behalf of the patient. (A Durable Power of Attorney for Health Care is included in the Personal Medical Mandate on pages 63–69.)

Eighteen states (and the District of Columbia) have statutes that permit agents designated by a Durable Power of Attorney for Health Care to withdraw or withhold life support:

California	Mississippi	South Dakota
Georgia	Nevada	Tennessee
Illinois	Ohio	Texas
Kansas	Oregon	Vermont
Kentucky	Rhode Island	West Virginia
Maine	South Carolina	Wisconsin
District of Columbia		

Seven states have Durable Powers of Attorney for Health Care that authorize agents to consent to medical treatment but do not specifically authorize them to allow withdrawal or withholding of life support: Alaska, Colorado, Connecticut, New Mexico, North Carolina, Pennsylvania, and Washington. And eight states have Durable Powers of Attorney for Health Care that through court decision or other means have been *interpreted* to permit agents to make medical decisions, including withholding or withdrawing life support: Arizona, Colorado, Hawaii, Iowa, Maryland, New Jersey, New York, and Virginia.

Some states include a checklist that expresses specific guidelines for the named guardian. Rhode Island, for example, allows a person to indicate the following:

By way of example, I have indicated by my initials in each of the categories below my desires by specifically authorizing my agent to act or by specifically prohibiting my agent from acting in the following categories. As to any matter in which I have not expressed any desire or limitation, I grant to my agent full power and authority as set forth in paragraph 3 of the Statutory Form Durable Power of Attorney for Health Care.

1. My agent may/may not arrange for my placement in or removal from any hospital, convalescent home, hospice, or other medical facility.

2. My agent may/may not require that medical treatment that only prolongs my inevitable death or irreversible coma (including, by way of example but not of limitation, such treatment as cardiopulmonary resuscitation, surgery, dialysis, use of a respirator, blood transfusions, antibiotics, antiarrhythmic and pressor drugs, or transplants) not be instituted or, if previously instituted, be discontinued.

3. My agent may/may not require, if I am in an irreversible coma with no reasonable possibility of my ever regaining consciousness, that procedures used to provide me with nourishment and hydration (including by way of example but not of limitation, parenteral feeding, intravenous feeding, misting, and endotracheal or nasogastric tube use) not be instituted or, if previously instituted, be discontinued.

4. My agent may/may not consent to and arrange for administration of pain-relieving drugs of any kind or other surgical or medical procedures calculated to relieve any pain, including unconventional or nonstandard pain-relief therapies that may be helpful, even though such drugs or procedures may have adverse side effects, may cause addiction, or may hasten the moment of (but not intentionally cause) my death.

5. My agent may/may not authorize experimental medical treatment if such treatment may conceivably result in an improvement in my medical condition even though such procedures may not yet be standard medical practice or if the possible primary result of such treatment may be additional scientific data on conditions similar to mine.

This kind of detailed instruction can be helpful for the agent in understanding the wishes of the patient and relieves the agent of some of the difficulty of withdrawing artificial life-prolonging procedures.

Whether through a health care proxy or a Durable Power of Attorney for Health Care, the law does permit a designated person to act on a patient's behalf. Further, the law has recognized this right even when no advance directive was provided. In this case the right is based on the principle of "substituted judgment." No one, however, should depend only on this far weaker protection.

THE STORY OF JOSEPH SAIKEWICZ

Joseph Saikewicz had an IQ of 10 and had been profoundly retarded all his life, most of which had been spent institutionalized. When he was sixty-seven he was diagnosed to be suffering from leukemia. His court-appointed guardian argued that he should not have to undergo chemotherapy, which would have been the normal procedure. The argument was made on the basis that it had only a fair chance of success at his age, that the effects would be debilitating, and that Saikewicz would not understand what was happening.

The court agreed with the guardian and affirmed the principle of substituted judgment, but it made clear that treatment was not to be denied because of handicaps.

The Saikewicz decision was criticized because it suggested that the court was the appropriate seat for decisions of this kind, as opposed to the physician or hospital ethics committee in concert with the patient and family. The case was significant because it extended individual autonomy to people who are unable to exercise it by themselves and who must rely on a proxy.

Personal Medical Mandate

A Personal Medical Mandate is a variant of a Living Will that details more specifically what treatments the patient does and does not want in the event he or she cannot communicate those instructions. In June 1989 two physicians proposed this new type of advance care document in the *Journal of the American Medical Association*. Its purpose was to provide greater specificity to help physicians understand the wishes of patients. The authors, Linda and Ezekiel Emanuel, argued that "the most important operational terms [of many Living Wills]—'no reasonable expectation of . . . recovery,' 'heroic measures,' 'life prolonging procedures,' etc.—are open to multiple interpretations on when to act and on what interventions the patient would desire."

———

In concert with the ethics committee of my (Hersh's) local hospital, we have created a similar document. The disadvantage of this type of medical directive in a national application is that legislated language regarding advance care directives is not standardized, and many states have mandated their own particular wording. Nonetheless, many physicians would be better able to ease the passage with such a document in place, in addition to a Living Will.

———

We recommend that readers execute a Personal Medical Mandate. It provides the most comprehensive set of directives in a single document. It is a Living Will, a Durable Power of Attorney for Health Care, and an elaboration of specific wishes in matters of wanted and unwanted treatments.

As suggested on page 50, there is a reason for executing a simple, generic Living Will in addition to one that is state-specific, depending on residency. The Personal Medical Mandate requires more effort to complete. Perhaps especially for a younger person in good health, however, it presents a vehicle for clearly indicating in advance wishes for medical treatment at any moment thereafter that it is impossible to express them verbally. A further advantage of the Personal Medical Mandate is that it encourages a physician-patient discussion of future options, and it provides care givers, family, and those empowered by a Durable Power of Attorney for Health Care specific guidelines on a patient's wishes. The document opens with strong language concerning the significance of the content.

The Personal Medical Mandate requires some amplification. First, it does not supersede the language of a state's Living Will legislation, but it can support it.

Second, it is beneficial to complete the optional sections on additional treatment that is wanted or not wanted while in consultation with a physician, because the implications of these instructions should be understood. For example, if untreated by antibiotics, pneumonia may rapidly cause death. Aggressive treatment in some situations, even in patients diagnosed as being terminally ill, may secure additional quality time for that patient. In other circumstances, pneumonia would be a welcome aid to easing the passage. The wish for a Hospice referral, as another example, provides an alternative regimen of care that is focused on comfort measures and symptom and pain control, not on cure of the underlying disease which has been diagnosed as terminal.

Third, the personal statement has an important function. Because Living Wills continue to evolve in their language and application, there are still going to be times when the physician or agent must wonder "Exactly what would my patient want me to do at this moment?" At the same time, it may be difficult for a designated agent to make a judgment that is clear of his or her own emotional bias. In the case of a spouse acting as the designated agent, this can be particularly stressful if the withholding or withdrawal of life-supporting treatment is involved. The wrenching truth of this was revealed in the six-hour PBS documentary "Near Death." Disease-tortured terminally ill patients were subjected to increasingly invasive procedures, the result of which was only to prolong death a few days. The next of kin could bring themselves only to ask the physicians to do everything to save their loved ones. A Personal Medical Mandate that addresses these questions will better allow wishes to be honored.

Finally, it must be understood that a Living Will, a deputized agent, and a Personal Medical Mandate come into play *only* when a patient is unable to make an informed judgment. These documents never preempt the decisions and consent of a competent patient. Furthermore, they may be revoked or changed at any time by the signer. They do, however, affirm one's control of one's destiny, and as suggested in the opening chapter, they remove the common fear of a lingering and painful death, thereby improving the quality of life.

PERSONAL MEDICAL MANDATE
(including a Durable Power of Attorney for Health Care)

Prefatory Warning

This is an important legal document. Consider this matter carefully. Under common law, you have the right to refuse unwanted treatment and you may request the care you do want, but under certain medical conditions you may not be capable of expressing yourself at the critical time. In such situation, the directive to your physician gives you the opportunity to express yourself by spelling out your wishes *in advance*.

You may list specific life-prolonging treatments that you do not want. In addition, there may be specific instructions or concerns (such as regarding pain control or types of nursing care) that you may wish to communicate. This Mandate also provides for you to designate another person to act on your behalf by making medical decisions if you cannot speak for yourself and ensuring that your directions and wishes are carried out.

Before executing this document, you should know these important facts:

You must be at least eighteen (18) years of age for this document to be legally valid and binding.

This Mandate gives the person you designate as your agent (the attorney-in-fact) the power to make health decisions for you. Your agent must act consistently with your desires as stated in this document.

Except as you otherwise specify in this document, this Mandate gives your agent the power to consent to your doctor, withholding treatment or stopping treatment necessary to keep you alive.

Notwithstanding this Mandate, you have the right to make medical and other health care decisions for yourself so long as you can give informed consent with respect to the particular decision. In addition, no treatment may be given to you over your objection at the time, and health care necessary to keep you alive may not be stopped or withheld if you object at the time.

This Mandate gives your agent authority to consent, to refuse consent, or to withdraw consent to any care, treatment, service, or procedure to maintain, diagnose, or treat a physical or mental condition. This power is subject to any statement of your desires and any limitation that you include in this document. You may state in this Mandate any types of treatment that you do not desire. In addition, a court can take away the power of your agent to make health care decisions for you if your agent (1) authorizes anything that is illegal, (2) acts contrary to your known desires, or (3) where your desires are not known, does anything that is clearly contrary to your best interests.

Unless you specify a specific period, this power will exist until you revoke it. Your agent's power and authority ceases upon your death.

You have the right to revoke the authority of your agent by notifying your agent or your treating doctor, hospital, or other health care provider orally or in writing of the revocation.

Your agent has the right to examine your medical records and to consent to their disclosure unless you limit this right in this document.

This document revokes any prior Durable Power of Attorney for Health Care.

You should carefully read and follow the witnessing procedure described at the end of this form. This document will not be valid unless you comply with the witnessing procedure.

If there is anything in this Mandate that you do not understand, you should ask a lawyer and your physician to explain it to you.

Durable Power of Attorney for Health Care

By this document I intend to create a Durable Power of Attorney for Health Care by appointing the person designated below to make health care decisions for me as allowed by law.

This power of attorney shall not be affected by my subsequent incapacity.

I, _____, do hereby designate and appoint _____ as my attorney-in-fact (agent) to make health care decisions for me as authorized in this document.

Address: _____
_____

Telephone: _____

If I become incapable of giving informed consent to health care decisions, I hereby grant to my agent full power and authority to make health care decisions for me including the right to consent, refuse consent, or withdraw consent to any care, treatment, service, or procedure to maintain, diagnose or treat a physical or mental condition, and to receive and to consent to the release of medical information, subject to the statement of desire, special provisions, and limitations set out elsewhere in this document.

When necessary to implement the health care decisions that my agent is authorized by this document to make, my agent has the power and authority to execute on my behalf all of the following:

(a) Documents entitled or purporting to be a "Refusal to Permit Treatment" and "Leaving Hospital against Medical Advice."

(b) Any necessary waiver or release from liability required by a hospital or physician.

If the person listed above is unavailable or unwilling to make a health care decision for me, then I designate the following persons to serve as my agent to make health care decisions for me as authorized in this document, such persons to serve in the order listed below:

Name: _____

Address: _____
_____

Telephone: _____

Name: _____

Address: _____
_____

Telephone: _____

I sign my name to this Durable Power of Attorney for Health Care on _____ at _____ , _____ .

    (date)   (city)   (state)

_____
Signature

Statement of Witnesses

I declare under penalty of perjury under the laws of my state that the person who signed or acknowledged this document is personally known to me to be the principal; that the principal signed or acknowledged this Durable Power of Attorney for Health Care in my presence; that the principal appears to be sound of mind and under no duress, fraud, or undue influence; that I am not the person appointed as attorney-in-fact by this document; and that I am not a health care provider, an employee of a health care provider, the operator of a community care facility or residential care facility for the elderly, nor an employee of an operator of a community facility or residential care facility for the elderly.

Signature _____ Address_____

Print name _____ _____

Date _____ _____

Signature _____ Address_____

Print name _____ _____

Date _____ _____

At least one of the above witnesses must also sign the following declaration:

I further declare under penalty of perjury under the laws of my state that I am not related to the principal by blood, marriage, or adoption, and, to the best of my knowledge I am not entitled to any part of the estate of the principal upon the death of the principal under a will now existing or by operation of law.

Signature _____   Address_____
Print name _____   _____
Date   _____   _____

Signature _____   Address_____
Print name _____   _____
Date   _____   _____

Specific Directives

NOTE: The signer may delete any of the following three preambles not agreed to.

If I am in a persistent vegetative state or a coma and in the opinion of my physician(s) have little or no hope of surviving or regaining awareness and higher mental functions no matter what is done,

—or—

If I have brain damage or some brain disease that cannot be reversed and that makes me unable to recognize people or to speak understandably, *but I have no terminal illness,* and can live in this condition for a long time,

—or—

If I have a terminal illness, such as incurable cancer, that will likely be the cause of my death,

this Personal Medical Mandate expresses, and shall stand for, my wishes regarding medical treatments in the event that illness should make me unable to communicate them directly. My initials below indicate my wishes regarding the use of the following:

1 Cardiopulmonary resuscitation—if on the point of dying, the use of drugs, chest compression, electric shock to start the heart beating, and artificial breathing. I

_____   _____   _____
      Want   Do not want   Undecided

66

2 Mechanical ventilation—breathing by machine. I

_____   _____   _____
   Want   Do not want   Undecided

3 Artificial nutrition and hydration—nutrition and fluid given through a tube in the veins, nose, or stomach. I

_____   _____   _____   _____
 Want   Do not want   Undecided   Trial; stop if
no improvement

4 Major surgery—such as removing part of the intestines, amputation of limbs. I

_____   _____   _____
   Want   Do not want   Undecided

5 Kidney dialysis—cleaning the blood by machine or by fluid passed through the stomach. I

_____   _____   _____   _____
 Want   Do not want   Undecided   Trial; stop if
no improvement

6 Chemotherapy—drugs to fight cancer. I

_____   _____   _____   _____
 Want   Do not want   Undecided   Trial; stop if
no improvement

7 Minor surgery—such as removing some tissue from an infected toe. I

_____   _____   _____
   Want   Do not want   Undecided

8 Invasive diagnostic tests—such as using a flexible tube to look into the stomach. I

_____   _____   _____
   Want   Do not want   Undecided

9 Blood or blood products. I

_____   _____   _____   _____
 Want   Do not want   Undecided   Trial; stop if
no improvement

10 Antibiotics—drugs to fight infection. I

Want	Do not want	Undecided	Trial; stop if no improvement

11 Simple diagnostic tests—such as blood tests or x rays. I

Want	Do not want	Undecided

12 Pain medications—even if they dull consciousness and indirectly shorten my life. I

Want	Do not want	Undecided

You may list specific treatment you do *not* want, in addition to the above items—for example, treatment in an intensive care unit (ICU).

I especially do not want:

_____
_____
_____
_____
_____
_____
_____
_____

You may want to add instructions for care you *do* want—for example, Hospice referral or that you prefer to die at home, if possible.

Other instructions:

_____
_____
_____
_____
_____
_____
_____
_____
_____
_____

Organ Donation

Pursuant to the Uniform Anatomical Gift Act, I hereby make this anatomical gift to take effect upon my death.

I give

_____ my body

_____ any needed organs or parts

The following organs or parts: _____

_____

for the following purposes:

_____ any purpose authorized by law

_____ transplantation

_____ therapy

_____ research

_____ medical education

Personal Statement

My personal statement:

_____

_____

_____

_____

_____

_____

_____

Signature

_____

Date

Copies

Your agent may need this document *IMMEDIATELY* in case of an emergency that requires a decision concerning your health care. You should keep the completed original document and give a copy of it to your agent and any alternative agents. You should also give a copy to your doctor, members of your family, and any other people who would likely need a copy of this form to carry out your wishes (such as the local ambulance service, your local hospital). Photocopies of this document can be relied on as though they were originals.

CHAPTER SIX

Easing the Passage:
Critical Definitions

To understand an individual's rights under law and medical ethics, one must be familiar with certain key phrases. Although they are largely self-explanatory, they contain important implications for obtaining constitutional rights in medical treatment. The courts—state and federal—wrestle with these definitions in right-to-die cases, and state legislatures make laws intended to clarify their meaning. It is important to understand these concepts when dealing with a hospital, physician, nurse, or other care giver because easing the passage can be accomplished or obstructed depending on an individual's command of these distinctions and ability to call for actions based on them.

This chapter refers frequently to the President's Commission. In 1983 the President's Commission for the Study of Ethical Problems in Medicine and Biomedical and Behavioral Research issued the results of an exhaustive study in a report called *Deciding to Forego Life-Sustaining Treatment: A Report on the Ethical, Medical, and Legal Issues in Treatment Decisions.* This book refers to it hereafter more simply as the President's Commission. The Commission was composed principally of experts in several fields of medicine and was chaired by the prestigious Doctor of Law and Jurisprudence Morris Abrams. Its findings are a document of humane persuasion and are detailed in their analysis of the many complex issues involved in the rights of dying people. The summary letter that accompanied its transmittal to then President Reagan read as follows:

Although our study has done nothing to decrease our estimation of the importance of this subject [death] to physicians, patients, and their families, we have concluded that the cases that involve true ethical difficulties are many fewer than commonly believed and that the perception of difficulties occurs primarily because of misunderstandings about the dictates of law and ethics. Neither criminal nor civil law precludes health care practitioners or their patients and relatives from reaching ethically and medically appropriate decisions about when to engage in or to forego efforts to sustain the lives of dying patients.

Applying the findings of our earlier study on informed consent, we have concluded that the authority of competent, informed patients to decide about their health care encompasses the decision to forego treatment and allow death to occur. We note, however, that all patients, including those who reject various forms of life-support, should receive other appropriate medical care to preserve their dignity and minimize suffering to the greatest extent possible.

When patients are incompetent to make their own decisions, others must act on their behalf. The Commission found that existing legal procedures can be adapted for the purpose of allowing people while competent to designate someone to act in their stead and to express their wishes about treatment. When it is not possible to know what a particular patient would have chosen—as, for example, with seriously ill infants—those who make the choices should attempt to serve the patient's best interests, judged from the patient's vantage point.

COMPETENT PATIENT. This term *should* be straightforward (see also autonomy and privacy in the glossary). It describes a person who has the mental faculty to understand options presented by a physician, to choose from among them, and to express that choice. Patients should not be declared incompetent just because they may choose to refuse an option that is considered medically sensible. The Supreme Court of the state of Washington decreed that "competency is *presumed;* to overcome this presumption, clear, cogent and convincing evidence is necessary" (emphasis added). The President's Commission states that the test of competency is that "the individual must have sufficiently stable and developed personal values and goals, an ability to communicate and understand information adequately, and an ability to reason and deliberate sufficiently well about the choices." It went on to state that these tests were not abrogated by other criteria even if decisions of requesting or foregoing life-sustaining therapies were involved. In other words, competency as a criterion for self-determination is not jeopardized by what attending health professionals may believe is an unwise decision. It is important to understand this as a patient's *right*. Because *the bias of medicine is so strongly for prolonging life, physicians have been tempted to bypass a patient's expressed wish on the grounds that he or she is not competent to make that decision.* The President's Commission goes on to make this right especially clear.

> A decision to forego such [life-prolonging] treatment is awesome because it hastens death, but that does not change the elements of decision-making capacity and need not require greater abilities on the part of a patient. Decisions about the length of life are not necessarily more demanding of a patient's capabilities than other important decisions. And decisions that might shorten life are not always regarded by patients as difficult ones: a patient who, even with treatment, has a very short time to live, may find a few additional hours rather unimportant, especially if the person has had a chance to take leave of loved ones and is reconciled to his or her situation.

In June 1990, Dr. Jack Kevorkian assisted Janet Adkins in committing suicide. The case received widespread attention in the national media, and Dr. Kevorkian quickly became tagged the "suicide doctor," and his programmed intravenous device, the "suicide machine." The immediate debate that erupted over this incident was on the ethical and legal question of whether a physician may assist in suicide (physician-assisted suicide and euthanasia are discussed in chapter 8). Buried in the news coverage of this incident was this question: was Adkins competent to make such a decision and to express such a wish? Because Dr. Kevorkian was not a psychologist, it was suggested he could not have been able to establish whether Janet Adkins was competent. Nowhere is it stated that competency must be evaluated and determined by specialists in psychology or psychiatry.

INFORMED CONSENT. Before a physician can perform a procedure or, in fact, even touch a person, he or she must obtain consent. This principle has a long legal grounding. In 1914 Justice Benjamin Cardozo wrote, "A human being of adult years and sound mind has a right to determine what shall be done with his body." This has become known as "Cardozo's root premise." The courts continue to uphold this principle. Physicians and even family members, however, continue to tamper with or blatantly violate the right to informed consent. An article in the *Journal of Legal Medicine*, "Informed Consent Statutes and the Decisionmaking Process," stated: "It may be that a patient will make an informed decision against undergoing a particular procedure that, once the person's condition deteriorates to be life-threatening, the physician may perform the procedure against the patient's will on the grounds that the situation was an emergency and informed consent was therefore not required."

THE STORY OF MRS. CANDURA

Mrs. Candura was seventy-seven years old. After her husband died, she continued to live at home but was depressed and unhappy. When part of her right foot was amputated she was no longer able to live alone. Gangrene, a disease characterized by the death of muscle and connective tissue due to a lack of circulation, subsequently developed in the rest of her foot and her leg. Untreated, gangrene spreads and can cause death. Candura's physician explained this to her and said he wanted to amputate her leg. She understood the consequences of not having the operation, and she also understood

*that the consequence of having it would be life as an invalid
in a nursing home. She refused.*

*Armed with a psychiatrist's testimony that Mrs. Candura
was not competent to make the decision, her daughter went
to court and asked that she be appointed her mother's guardian for the purpose of consenting to the operation. The psychiatrist's testimony made the case that the refusal to have
the operation was itself the proof of incompetence. The court
agreed, but Candura appealed. The appellate court ruled that
because she was aware of the consequences of her decision,
she was competent to make the choice to forego surgery. In its
decision the court stated: "Mrs. Candura's decision may be
regarded by most as unfortunate, but on the record in this
case it is not the uninformed decision of a person incapable of
appreciating the nature and consequence of her act. . . . We
are all of the opinion that the operation may not be forced on
her against her will."*

That an individual should have the right to approve amputation will seem rudimentary to most readers. The United
States Constitution grants us the right to privacy. Individual
autonomy is a protected gift, and to obtain it the *Mayflower*
first sailed to these shores in 1620. Yet in a strange acquies-
cence to experts, patients often say "All right, do what you
think is necessary." Often, they may not realize that they
have the *right* to forbid a physician to proceed.

While the right of informed consent gathers increasing
force in today's physician-patient relationships as a result of
public attention to the issue of the right to die, the medical
community is beginning to rumble that this right is being
stretched too far. In a prologue to an article on resuscitation
in the September 1990 *Journal of the American Medical Association*, it was stated:

Recent recommendations that physicians be allowed to
withhold cardiopulmonary resuscitation, without patient con-

sent, from patients for whom it would be futile have drawn objections that such unilateral judgments would undermine respect for patient autonomy. These objections assume that since futility determinations involve value judgments, patient input is always required. However, certain sorts of value judgments must be made unilaterally by physicians as part of reasonable medical practice. Moreover, the mixed messages inherent in requesting patient consent to withhold futile therapy serve to undermine rather than to enhance autonomous choice. Real patient interests can better be served by a broad public dialogue around judgments of medical reasonableness and medical futility, rather than concern for the form but not the substance of patient autonomy.

Although the premise of this article was purportedly to help ease the passage, the challenge to the principle of informed consent is nonetheless troubling. This is especially true in the context of health insurance parameters that may lead to a form of triage (discussed in chapter 4).

THE STORY OF ABE PERLMUTTER

Abe Perlmutter was a seventy-three-year-old man with amyotrophic lateral sclerosis (a degenerative disease of the nervous system, commonly known as Lou Gehrig's disease). He was paralyzed by the disease and needed to be permanently attached to a respirator to ventilate his lungs. Perlmutter was alert and competent, and with the concurrence of his family, he requested that the respirator be disconnected. The hospital refused on the ground that it might be liable for an act of homicide.

The court ruled that Perlmutter had a constitutional right to refuse or discontinue medical therapy, and that to continue against his wish constituted an invasion of his right to privacy.

The respirator was disconnected and Perlmutter died shortly thereafter.

Informed consent provides a competent patient the legal right to refuse treatment even if foregoing that treatment will hasten death. In other words, no medical procedure may be undertaken unless agreed to by the patient. Informed consent does *not* allow a patient to insist on a treatment that medical ethics would consider unacceptable. Some procedures are not undertaken by a physician without a patient's having signed a release indicating informed consent. This consent also absolves the physician of certain liabilities if risks in the procedure become reality. Often this informed consent is obtained in a routine and casual way. A patient, for example, enters the hospital for an appendectomy. Before going into surgery he or she is given a form to sign indicating consent to the operation. Certain other actions, however, may be taken without this written agreement, for example, the placement of an intravenous tube for delivering medications.

At a time of easing the passage, informed consent can become confused in two ways: by the way the consent is requested by a physician and by procedures that may be initiated without informed consent at all. The President's Commission stated:

> One of the things that patients rightly expect from professionals, and that professionals usually expect to provide, is advice rather than neutral information about treatment options and their risks and benefits. However, the way advice is provided can vary substantially. Individual personality styles, both of the professional and of the patient, range from authoritarian through nondirective.

In other words, a patient or the family may be "sold" by a physician on a procedure because the physician believes that it is the appropriate medical procedure. Although true, such a rationale ignores what may be the patient's desire not to prolong a terminal illness. Thus the way informed consent is solicited can vary, with significant consequence for the patient. The following case illustrates this point.

THE STORY OF JIM GRAY

Jim Gray, ninety-one, suffered his third heart attack at home and was brought to the hospital in an ambulance. He was placed in the intensive care unit (ICU). Through the intravenous administration of a number of medications, his condition stabilized. After a series of blood tests it was discovered that the heart attack had been major and that the heart muscle had sustained significant permanent damage. The admitting physician described this situation to Gray and told him that the prognosis was uncertain—he might live a year, or his heart might arrest while he was still in the hospital. The physician then asked Gray, "Should your heart stop while you are in the hospital, do you wish us to undertake resuscitation procedures?" The physician explained how this would be attempted and that these efforts had no guarantee of being successful, but might be. Jim Gray's answer was considered, and even philosophical. He did not want resuscitation, he said, because "when my heart stops, that is nature saying it is over." After that conversation, a do-not-resuscitate order was written on Gray's chart.

A second physician, however, who succeeded the first one in Gray's care in the hospital, went through the conversation again and presented the question differently. He stated that resuscitation was as simple a procedure as taking blood pressure and that any shock treatment would occur quickly enough so that there would be no side effects. He argued for this procedure in such a persuasive, almost jovial way that Gray agreed that the attempt could be made to restart his heart should it arrest. "Just sign this, Jim," the doctor said, "just to prove that you know what you are saying." Gray managed to make a squiggle on the consent document. When asked by Gray's family why he had made the case for resuscitation in such a subjective manner, the second physician responded, "Because I think he has some good quality time left." In fact, those who knew Jim Gray well were aware that he had frequently stated he was ready to die, and just "wanted to die in his sleep."

The reason that this case is important for a reader is that the second physician had a predetermined bias that could *not* have been based on the facts. He knew nothing of Jim Gray's life, had met him only in the context of the ICU. Whether the consent obtained was *informed* is in doubt. It is cast further into doubt by the fact that Gray had executed both a Living Will and a Durable Power of Attorney for Health Care that stated that he did *not* want resuscitation. At this point the definitions of *competent* and *informed consent* come together over the following question: if Jim Gray made those advance directives while competent, should they be persuasively altered as he lay feeble and disoriented in the ICU? There is no answer to the question, except had Gray been under Hospice care because of his debilitating heart disease (see chapter 9), a do-not-resuscitate order would have remained in force.

The principle of informed consent by a competent patient is today legally and ethically well established. The right to privacy and patient autonomy underpin the principle. It therefore is one of the most important tools in easing the passage. Neither a physician nor a hospital may compel a terminally ill patient to receive treatment. As the cases of Mrs. Candura and Abe Perlmutter illustrate, however, it unfortunately sometimes takes considerable effort to enforce this principle. (These cases took place in the 1970s. Since then, there has been a marked change in bioethical attitudes on the subject, and the medical community is more sensitive to the right of patients' autonomy. Note, however, that the story of Jim Gray took place in 1990.)

ASSAULT AND BATTERY. A common law term, assault and battery is what a physician can legally be charged with if he proceeds with a treatment that has been refused by the patient or by the patient's legally appointed agent. Battery is an unpermitted touching of the body. If not consented to, insertion of an intravenous tube is battery. Assault is the fear-producing threat of battery. A physician who states he is going to insert an intravenous tube without the patient's permission has committed an assault.

ACTS AND OMISSIONS (THAT LEAD TO DEATH). Acts are further subdivided between withdrawing and withholding treatment. A physician who administers a lethal injection of poison to a dying person has committed murder under existing law. That is an act. If a layperson throws gasoline on someone and ignites it, killing the person, that also is an *act* of murder. If, however, the same layperson comes on someone caught in a conflagration and does not attempt to extricate the person, that *omission to act* is not murder.

For a professional, omission carries a greater weight. If a fireman on the above scene stood by and did nothing, he or she would be criminally liable. So too, a physician may be in legal difficulty if he or she fails to apply an appropriate treatment. This becomes a gray area in both law and medical ethics: on what criteria is omission acceptable? A physician who does not control bleeding from a laceration has violated his responsibility, but a physician who fails to order surgery for a patient near death has acted responsibly. The President's Commission argued these distinctions:

> In both scholarly and policy discussions, "killing" is often equated with an action causing death, and "allowing to die" an omission causing death. Killing and allowing to die are then used as merely descriptive terms, leaving open which actual actions that cause death are morally wrong. . . . In an attempt to avoid confusion that stems from these conflicting usages and to present the important issues clearly, the Commission's discussion employs the terms actions—that lead to death and omissions that lead to death. . . . The distinction between a fatal act and a fatal omission depends upon the difference between a person physically acting and refraining from acting and upon what might be called the background

course of events. . . . Sometimes deciding whether a particular course involves an act of an omission is less clear. Stopping a respirator at the request of a competent patient who could have lived with it for a few years but who will die without it in just a few hours is such an ambiguous case. Does the physician omit continuing the treatment or act to disconnect it? Discontinuing essential dialysis treatments or choosing not to give the next in a sequence of antibiotic doses are events that could be described either as acts or omissions.

These distinctions have been thrashed around in the courts and in committees of medical ethics. They are important because the reader must understand that no one can ask a physician to commit an act that will kill. With informed consent, however, a competent patient, or a legally designated agent, can have a physician act or not act in accordance with the patient's wishes, and a physician's right does not normally exceed that wish, even if death is a foreseeable consequence of that act or omission to act. A physician who proceeds to act in contrary to that wish is in violation of an individual's constitutional right to privacy.

Withdrawing and withholding treatment. These terms mean exactly what they appear to mean. However, they become laden with other considerations. Is not withholding treatment an omission and withdrawing it an act? And if it is generally easier to justify an omission, is there not a real difference between the two in terms of what can be done by a physician to ease the passage? The differentiation is further complicated by actual procedures. If a therapy requires repeated application, does stopping applications partway through the schedule constitute withholding or withdrawing? The reader needs to be familiar with these ambiguities because physicians can be less comfortable with withdrawing treatment when they know that it may constitute hastening the death of the patient. Yet to insist on a distinction for purposes of deciding on a program of care can work to the patient's disadvantage. A physician may hesitate to initiate a therapy that might be beneficial but probably will not initiate it if he or she is worried that withdrawing the treatment may be criticized. "Ironically," states the President's Commission,

> if there is any call to draw a moral distinction between withholding and withdrawing, it generally cuts the opposite way from the usual formulation: greater justification ought to be required to withhold than withdraw treatment. Whether a particular treatment will have positive effects is often highly uncertain before the therapy has been tried. If a trial of therapy makes clear that it is not helpful to the patient, this is actual evidence (rather than mere surmise) to support stopping because the therapeutic benefit that earlier was a possibility has been found to be clearly unobtainable. . . . Given that the Commission considers as unwarranted the view that steps leading to death are always more serious when they involve an act rather than an omission, it also rejects the view that stopping a treatment ("an act") is morally more serious than not starting it ("an omission") could be. . . . The distinction between failing to initiate and stopping therapy—that is, withholding versus withdrawing treatment—is not itself of moral importance. A justification that is adequate for not commencing a treatment is also sufficient for ceasing it. Moreover, erecting a higher requirement for cessation might unjustifiably discourage vigorous initial attempts to treat seriously ill patients that sometimes succeed.

———

Nonetheless, it is psychologically more difficult for a physician to withdraw than to withhold a treatment. Even though I (Hersh) am in full agreement with the President's Commission's view on the matter, I find it more comfortable to withhold a form of therapy than to initiate it and then withdraw it when the medical situation is hopelessly deteriorating.

———

Part of Nancy Cruzan's case centered on the distinction between these alternatives of withholding and withdrawing. Before it had been determined by the hospital that the extended deprivation of oxygen from her brain had caused permanent irreversible brain damage, the hospital requested and received permission from her family to surgically implant a feeding tube in her abdomen. That is to say, consent was given to initiate a procedure. When it was ultimately determined that with artificial feeding Cruzan could live for perhaps thirty years, but only in a persistent vegetative state, her parents asked that the feeding tube be *withdrawn*. The state of Missouri initially denied this request.

INTENTIONAL VERSUS UNINTENTIONAL BUT WITH FORESEEABLE CONSEQUENCES. This is an important distinction when the consequence is likely to be death. A common medical example of this is in the administration of morphine. The dosage required to eliminate pain in a cancer victim may be sufficient to create a respiratory problem that hastens death. The physician foresees death, but because the intent is not to cause death but to relieve pain, the procedure is legal and ethical.

ORDINARY VERSUS EXTRAORDINARY TREATMENT. Two words that have equivalent meanings are often substituted for *extraordinary—artificial* and *heroic*.

As in all these definitions, there can be exceptions to their normal interpretation. In the dichotomy of ordinary versus extraordinary, however, the differences are very much narrowed in the case of dying patients. Treatments routinely used during surgery and other therapies that *cure* might be defined as ordinary. When, however, their employment can be characterized only as prolonging death, they cease to be ordinary.

In the context of a terminally ill patient, extraordinary, artificial, or heroic procedures include such things as major surgery and mechanical ventilation. Here, then, lies one of the most important reasons for executing a Living Will and a Durable Power of Attorney for Health Care: a competent patient has the right to accept or refuse these treatments. Without a clear prior statement of wishes or without a legally appointed spokesperson, however, a person unable to communicate may well be subjected to a number of extraordinary, aggressive, life-sustaining measures without consent (assault and battery).

DO-NOT-RESUSCITATE (DNR) ORDER (ALSO KNOWN AS A NO-CODE ORDER).
Emergency teams, paramedics, ambulance crews, and hospital staffs are all trained in resuscitation techniques. More than that, resuscitation is standard procedure, unless specifically indicated otherwise. In a hospital the order for resuscitation is referred to by the terms "full code" and "code blue." A heart stops, and a team of specialists goes to work trying to restart it. For this *not* to happen, a physician has to write a do-not-resuscitate (DNR), or no-code, order on the patient's chart. In other words, resuscitation is the automatic procedure unless preordered otherwise. The *Western Journal of Medicine* recently presented a framework to aid a physician in deciding whether to implement a DNR order:

1 If the patient is competent, honor his wishes.
2 If the patient is unable to understand his condition or express his wishes, establish the likelihood of reversing the illness:

a / If the illness is reversible, do not issue a DNR order.
b / If the prognosis is unclear, do not issue a DNR order.
c / If the illness is irreversible, a DNR order may be considered.

Note that the bias is for resuscitation, which may be appropriate in many instances but is less so in the case of terminally ill patients. The question raised for the physician in item 2 is answered if the patient has executed advance medical directives. Commenting on DNR orders, the American Academy of Family Practitioners made the additional point that "family members may disagree with the patient's decision to forego resuscitation. The opinions of family members are of concern to all involved ... nevertheless they do not override the informed, considered opinion of a competent, adult patient."

It is important for readers to understand to secure the agreement that there is to be *no* resuscitation requires a specific action on the part of the physician, who in turn will likely write this order only on the specific demand of the patient or the designated agent if the patient is unable to express the wish verbally. One hospital defines the acceptance of a DNR order as follows:

> The circumstances surrounding the no-code order will be documented in the progress notes. Documentation must include but not be limited to:
> A. A summary of the medical situation
> B. The outcome of consultation with other physicians
> C. A statement summarizing outcome of consultations with patient, guardian, conservator, or family
> D. The giving of informed consent to the patient, guardian, conservator or all members of the immediate family shall be clearly documented in the progress notes.
> All no-code orders shall be considered invalid after seventy-two hours and shall be reordered on the physicians' order sheet noting date and time. CPR will be initiated automatically if there is no written and signed no-code order on the order sheet. No nurse shall accept a verbal no-code order.

Dr. David Schiedermayer has described the "downside to *presumed* consent" as "futility in some cases, and undesired intervention in others. Nonetheless, because of their negative connotations, do-not-resuscitate orders are normally not discussed until too late, when the decision may be left to family members who are likely to be ambivalent." *Easing the Passage* has repeatedly argued for early written directives on this matter. They avoid the time of extremis and also what may be an inappropriate moment. "If I go in for hernia surgery," says Dr. Schiedermayer, "and the doctor says we have to talk about code status [DNR instructions], I'm going to ask to see his diploma."

THE STORY OF EDWARD WINTER

This case received front-page attention in 1990 for its unique twist in the right-to-die litigation literature when Edward Winter filed for damages resulting from having been resuscitated. Winter, in advance, had expressly rejected resuscitation. He had made these instructions clear to his physician and his daughters. His wife was dead, but before she died she had been resuscitated, which resulted in brain damage. Winter did not want that history repeated in his own case.

In May 1988, the eighty-two-year-old Winter collapsed with chest pains. He told his physician he did not wish to be resuscitated, and the physician wrote a DNR on his medical chart. Nonetheless, when Edward Winter suffered a cardiac arrest a few days later in the hospital, he was revived. Shortly thereafter he suffered an incapacitating stroke. Aware that his orders had been ignored, he retained an attorney to sue the hospital for its failure to follow his and its own—through the patient's chart—directive. Edward Winter has since died, but the case is proceeding on his behalf.

The importance of familiarity with the definitions in this chapter cannot be overemphasized. In many cases, until medical training and practice have caught up with existing ethics and laws, the patient or a designated surrogate may have to both interpret and control the situation.

———

Even with the knowledge gained in the research and writing of this book it took actual confrontation with medical personnel on my (Outerbridge's) part to help ease the passage of a dying relative. My eighty-five-year-old father had entered the hospital with a series of problems. He had a history of increasingly debilitating heart attacks and minor strokes. Now he was having difficulty breathing and was aspirating (fluid entered lungs upon swallowing). He was extremely weak. His physicians diagnosed a tumor in his throat as the cause of the breathing and swallowing problems. They asked for permission to perform a biopsy of the tumor to see if it was, as they believed, malignant. This was granted, but then they proceeded to perform a tracheostomy (something they had said would not be done without consultation). By that action, my father lost the ability to speak and was truly miserable. Forty-eight hours later, as I arrived on the scene, two other things happened. First, the physicians reported that the biopsy specimen had been taken from an inflammation rather than the tumor and stated that the operation would have to be repeated. Second, because my father could not swallow, a resident had asked him if a tube could be inserted into his nostril and down into his stomach to provide nutrition. "Consent" for this was obtained by saying, "Ken, we want to get you some nourishment, and would like to set this up artificially, which is going to make you feel much better." That sounded reasonable, so my poor father nodded agreement. When they were unable to ram the tube down one nostril they tried the other, which also was unsuccessful. I walked in the door at that moment. My father wrote the situation down for me. They had also told him they wanted to do the second biopsy. "This is terrible, terrible," my father wrote. I explained what was coming up next and asked if he wanted it, because he had an absolute right to refuse. My father then wrote on his yellow pad, "The doctor is an asshole, the doctor is an asshole."

I explained that without nutrition he was going to die. "That is fine," he wrote. I went through the scenario with him, pointing out that he would become increasingly weak, would sleep more, and at some point would die in his sleep. He nodded affirmatively to each element of the progression. Not trusting the hospital staff, I called witnesses into the room and repeated the entire conversation. I was emphatic, with his concurring nods, that the only things that were to be done for him were to provide comfort.

Once that was done a change came over my father. He became peaceful, and a virtual aura of tranquility replaced his agitated and nervous state. That night pneumonia developed and was treated only for comfort. My father died peacefully twelve hours later. Quite obviously, I should have been there earlier to preempt some preventable misery. But it was only my presence, armed with the knowledge of informed consent, patient autonomy, and so forth, that prevented another regimen of torturous procedures that would only have prolonged his time of dying.

———

Even courts can err on the question of who is in charge and who has the final word. The following story is an example.

THE STORY OF SHIRLEY DINNERSTEIN

Shirley Dinnerstein was sixty-seven, suffered from Alzheimer's disease, and was living in a vegetative state. She had serious coronary artery disease and high blood pressure. She also was incontinent and unable to swallow without aspirating food and liquid into her lungs. Dinnerstein's family and physician wished to enter a DNR order on her medical chart. Because of another case, it was suggested that such a decision had to be made by the court. The appellate court that heard the case determined that "what measures are appropriate to ease the imminent passing of an irreversibly, terminally ill patient" were the province of medical competence, not the judicial system.

This ruling is contrary to the principle of patient autonomy. It merely substituted the physician for the court. As another court ruled: "It is now a well-established rule of general law . . . that it is the patient, not the physician, who ultimately decides if treatment—any treatment—is to be given at all. . . . The rule has never been qualified in its application by either the nature or purpose of the treatment, or the gravity of the consequences of acceding to or foregoing it." As has been amply illustrated by case stories, however, it may still be a lonely and difficult fight to obtain these rights. And yet, because of public exposure of the issues surrounding the right to die, a new humanism is slowly creeping into behavior toward terminally ill patients. Nonetheless, for ordinary citizens, it is still almost essential that they be armed with the information in this book.

CHAPTER SEVEN

Easing the Passage: The Patient's Bill of Rights

> What tormented Ivan Ilych most was the deception, the lie, which for some reason they all accepted, that he was not dying but was simply ill, and that he only need keep quiet and undergo a treatment and then something very good would result. He however knew that do what they would nothing would come of it, only still more agonizing suffering and death. This deception tortured him— their not wishing to admit what they all knew and what he knew.
>
> —LEO TOLSTOY,
> "The Death of Ivan Ilych"

The American Hospital Association created the Patient's Bill of Rights to set a standard for hospitals. Copyrighted in 1975 by the association, it contains twelve principles. These principles, in addition to the various patient rights that exist under the law, should be kept in mind.

1 *The patient has the right to considerate and respectful care.* This seems so obvious. Hospitals are run from an institutional mentality, however. Good people are not necessarily good patients. Good people—strong in personality, skeptical, and argumentative—may be infuriating patients. A hospital tries to standardize everything, and like the military, which shaves everyone's head and issues uniform clothing, hospitals want their patients to be virtually the same in clothing and temperament and compliance.

2 *The patient has the right to obtain from his physician complete current information concerning his diagnosis, treatment, and prognosis in terms the patient can be reasonably expected to understand. When it is not medically advisable to give such information to the patient, the information should be made* *available to an appropriate person in his behalf. He has the right to know by name the physician responsible for coordinating his care.*

There are two points in this principle. First, the right to know of one's condition. The truth is important, and patients usually know when they are being fooled. On the other hand, bad news is often best delivered in stages. People can assimilate only fragments of the truth in some situations.

———

I (Hersh) have sat in a room with someone and told them, "You have a cancer in your lung," and they have walked out the door without knowing what I had said. The human mechanism of denial is very strong, so the medical vocabulary must often be upgraded gradually.

———

Yet there is nothing more cruel than leaving a patient *waiting* for current information. A biopsy is performed on Wednesday, the result is back on Friday, but the patient is not informed until Monday. As bad as the information may be, not providing that information immediately is unconscionable.

The second element of this principle is the right to know the responsible physician. It may be hard to imagine that obtaining the name of the physician in charge of your care would be a problem, but it can be in a large hospital if someone is unexpectedly admitted: who's in charge? Who is this person whose name is on the bracelet on my wrist?

3 *The patient has the right to receive from his physician information necessary to give informed consent prior to the start of any procedure and/or treatment. Except in emergencies, such information for informed consent should include, but not necessarily be limited to, the specific procedure and/or treatment, the medically significant risks involved, and the probable duration of incapacitation. Where medically significant alternatives for care or treatment exist, or when the patient requests infor-*

mation concerning medical alternatives, the patient has the right to such information. The patient also has the right to know the name of the person responsible for the procedures and/or treatment.

Today we have such an arsenal of therapies, and we can intrude on the natural process in so many ways, that often not enough thought goes into the consequences of alternative treatments or of foregoing therapy. Always the principle of beneficence should be in control of the options: "First, do no harm." What are the risks and the benefits attached to initiating a procedure or withholding it? Informed consent cannot be made without that review.

Although informed consent is required, it is often not even sought for many procedures, or it is made implicit. Doctors obtain it in writing before surgery and anesthesia for self-protection. Otherwise, it is often obtained in the most casual way, and the doctor has not fully advised the patient of the risks and benefits. Or consent is not obtained at all. A person contracts pneumonia, for example, and the doctor neither gets consent for intravenous administration of antibiotics before beginning it nor explains the consequences of not employing this therapy. For a terminally ill person, this is one of the occasions when the doctor can say to the patient or the family, "One of the options at this point is not using the antibiotic." What is the risk? It is death. But what is the benefit? A tranquil, quite rapid passage.

4 *The patient has the right to refuse treatment to the extent permitted by law, and to be informed of the medical consequences of his action.* "The extent permitted by law" is very wide. The only situation in which law does not permit refusal of treatment is under a public health arrest. People with communicable diseases (tuberculosis, for example) who fail to have them dealt with can be placed under a health arrest and treated. And courts can insist on therapy for children when parents refuse. A rare example of not being allowed to refuse treatment is described in the following story.

THE STORY OF ELIZABETH BOUVIA

Elizabeth Bouvia was born with cerebral palsy, which left her a bedridden quadriplegic. She was able to intentionally move only a few fingers of one hand and some facial muscles. Her muscle contractions and arthritis left her in a state of chronic pain. A tube was implanted in her chest for an automatic morphine administration. Nonetheless, Bouvia grew up, went to college, graduated, married, and became pregnant. She had a miscarriage, and her husband subsequently left her. She then lived under the care of her parents, until they were no longer able to manage. Without financial means, she could find nowhere to live where her extensive needs could be attended to.

In 1983 Elizabeth Bouvia sought admission to the Riverside General Hospital in California. There she refused to eat and began to starve herself to death. She requested that the hospital provide pain and comfort support. The hospital refused and indicated that it would insert a tube down her nose for forced feeding. Bouvia appealed to the court for an injunction against this. The court found that she had the right to end her life but that she had no right to require a third party, in this case the hospital, to assist her.

Bouvia then left the hospital. A number of social organizations tried to care for her on an at-home basis. She continued to starve herself, however, and her condition worsened. She was rehospitalized, this time at an institution run by the Department of Health Services. Aware of the previous court ruling, the hospital inserted a nasogastric tube against Bouvia's express written refusal of this treatment. She sought an injunction, this time from the court of appeals. This body defended her right to self-determination and ordered the tube removed.

The difference in the two court decisions was one of interpretation.

5 *The patient has the right to every consideration of his pri-*

vacy concerning his own medical care program. Case discussion, consultation, examination, and treatment are confidential and should be conducted discreetly. Those not directly involved in his care must have the permission of the patient to be present.

6 *The patient has the right to expect that all communications and records pertaining to his care should be treated as confidential.*

7 *The patient has the right to expect that within its capacity a hospital must make reasonable response to the request of a patient for services. The hospital must provide evaluation, service, and/or referral as indicated by the urgency of the case. When medically permissible a patient may be transferred to another facility only after he has received complete information and explanation concerning the needs for and alternatives to such a transfer. The institution to which the patient is to be transferred must first have accepted the patient for transfer.* Institution acceptance of transfer patients is now law. "Patient dumping" became a problem caused by hospital finances. Because of the dangers inherent in the transfer itself, hospitals are not allowed to transfer patients out because of their insurance status.

8 *The patient has the right to obtain information as to any relationship of his hospital to other health care and educational institutions insofar as his care is concerned. The patient has the right to obtain information as to the existence of any professional relationships among individuals, by name, who are treating him.*

9 *The patient has the right to be advised if the hospital proposes to engage in or perform human experimentation affecting his care or treatment. The patient has the right to refuse to participate in such research projects.*

10 *The patient has the right to expect reasonable continuity of care. He has the right to know in advance which appointment times and physicians are available and where. The patient has the right to expect that the hospital will provide a mechanism whereby he is informed by his physician or a delegate of the* *physician of the patient's continuing health care requirements following discharge.*

11 *The patient has the right to examine and receive an explanation of his bill regardless of source of payment.*

12 *The patient has the right to know which hospital rules and regulations apply to his conduct as a patient.* Examples include visiting hours and other restrictions placed on the patient and his family.

CHAPTER EIGHT

Easing the Passage:
Euthanasia

The more I have thought about these issues
the more I have become convinced that access to a humane death is one of the most
fundamental rights an individual should
have. Our Founding Fathers should have
written: "We hold these truths to be self-
evident . . . that all humans are endowed by
their creator with certain unalienable rights;
that among these are life, liberty, the pursuit
of happiness, and access to a humane death."
Surely, the denial of such a death is an assault on human dignity at least as egregious
as involuntary servitude or taxation without
representation or unreasonable searches and
seizures or all the myriad other intrusions
that the Founding Fathers sought to forbid.
In the absence of such a death, all citizens
are caged within the confines of life by their
fear of the process of dying.

—CALVIN SIMONDS,
Harvard Magazine

T he word *euthanasia* comes from the ancient Greek language: *eu* meaning "good" and *thanatos* meaning "death." In
modern-day usage, euthanasia has come to represent either
an active or a passive termination of a person's life. Because
of the historical connection of the word with the Nazi holo-
caust, it has a pejorative connotation as well.

The active termination of a person's life, for example, by
lethal injection, is against the law and against medical ethics.
In the few admitted cases of active euthanasia by physicians
in this country, prosecution for murder has often followed.
Euthanasia is also illegal in The Netherlands; as has been
widely reported by the media in the past, however, it is a
fairly common practice in that country. It is estimated that

more than five thousand patients die each year in The Netherlands through active euthanasia. Physicians there administer lethal injections openly, and because of a body of case law
and widespread public support, these instances are not prosecuted. The guidelines under which a physician can perform
euthanasia are narrowly drawn. First, the patient must be
competent. This condition would eliminate active euthanasia
for people such as Nancy Cruzan who are in persistent vegetative states. Second, the patient must request euthanasia
persistently over time, thereby eliminating the possibility for
someone who might be suffering from a temporary depression. Third, the patient must be suffering intolerably, with no
prospect of relief. (It is interesting, however, that a terminal
disease need not be involved.) Fourth, the procedure must by
performed by a physician after consultation and agreement
with another physician.

There are those within and outside the medical community
who argue that a similar policy should be legalized in the
United States. If it is appropriate to put a dying or suffering
animal out of its misery, should we not be able to do the same
for ourselves? The arguments against making euthanasia legal center on two points. The first is the fear that legalizing
"mercy killing" would open the door to abuse: that it could
become a way of killing unwanted people (the so-called slippery slope to abuse). The second argument is based on the
Hippocratic Oath: physicians should not be placed in the position of causing death; physicians must not kill.

On the other hand, death in three or four days through
starvation and dehydration—passive euthanasia, which is
both legal and ethical and is a standard way of easing a terminally ill patient out of the world at his or her request—is
not the most pleasant way to die. Once the decision to allow
death has been made between physician, patient, and family,
what is the ethical difference between giving a more painless,
tranquil (and currently illegal) death? Where is the slippery

slope to abuse *once* the decision has been made to permit death to occur under controlled circumstances?

People often ask the question of why it is normal, and considered completely appropriate, for a veterinarian to put an aged, suffering animal to sleep with a lethal injection but not appropriate for humans. The answer has to be that we are different from animals because we have classified ourselves as such—which creates a problem. A physician can morally, ethically, and legally allow someone to starve to death, and once that decision is made it is a *fait accompli*. Death is going to be allowed to take place over a few days. Would not that be the time for an instantaneous death by injection? A physician is extending the period of suffering by pulling tubes instead of administering injections.

Physicians do cause death on a covert basis at the request of dying patients, but no one wants to be the case study for a change in the law except grandstanders like Dr. Kevorkian. However, medical ethics is getting closer to an affirmative attitude toward active euthanasia. The ethical acceptance of passive euthanasia (withholding nutrition and hydration) or slow euthanasia (withdrawing them) pushes the physician closer to participating in the active form. As physicians see the discomfort that may be involved with a legally acceptable form of passive euthanasia, they must consider the next logical step. When they have crossed the line where they make the statement that they are going to do absolutely nothing for this person, the principle of beneficence needs to be invoked.

But it is against the law, which is the final answer at this point in our society.

In January 1988, an article appeared in the *Journal of the American Medical Association* titled "It's Over, Debbie."

The call came in the middle of the night. As a gynecology resident rotating through a large, private hospital, I had come to detest telephone calls, because invariably I would be up for several hours and would not feel good the next day. However, duty called, so I answered the phone. A nurse informed me that a patient was having difficulty getting rest, could I please see her. She was on 3 North. That was the gynecologic-oncology unit, not my usual duty station. As I trudged along, bumping sleepily against walls and corners and not believing I was up again, I tried to imagine what I might find at the end of my walk. Maybe an elderly woman with an anxiety reaction, or perhaps something particularly horrible.

I grabbed the chart from the nurses' station on my way to the patient's room, and the nurse gave me some hurried details: a 20-year-old girl named Debbie was dying of ovarian cancer. She was having unrelenting vomiting apparently as the result of an alcohol drip administered for sedation. Hmmm, I thought. Very sad. As I approached the room I could hear loud, labored breathing. I entered and saw an emaciated, dark-haired woman who appeared much older than 20. She was receiving oxygen, had an IV, and was sitting in bed suffering from what was obviously severe air hunger. The chart noted her weight at 80 pounds. A second woman, also dark-haired but of middle age, stood at her right, holding her hand. Both looked up as I entered. The room seemed filled with the patient's desperate effort to survive. Her eyes were hollow, and she had suprasternal and intercostal retractions with her rapid inspirations. She had not eaten or slept in two days. She had not responded to chemotherapy and was being given supportive care only. It was a gallows scene, a cruel mockery of her youth and unfulfilled potential. Her only words to me were, "Let's get this over with."

I retreated with my thoughts to the nurses' station. The patient was tired and needed rest. I could not give her health, but I could give her rest. I asked the nurse to draw 20 mg of morphine sulfate into a syringe. Enough, I thought, to do the job. I took the syringe into the room and told the two women I was going to give Debbie something that would let her rest and to say good-bye. Debbie looked at the syringe, then laid her head on the pillow with her eyes open, watching what was left of the world. I injected the morphine intravenously and watched to see if my calculations on its effects would be correct. Within seconds her breathing slowed to a normal rate, her eyes closed, and her features softened as she seemed restful at last. The older woman stroked the hair of the now-sleeping patient. I waited for the inevitable next effect of depressing the respiratory drive. With clocklike certainty, within four minutes the breathing rate slowed even more, then became irregular, then ceased. The dark-haired woman stood erect and seemed relieved.

It's over, Debbie.

It has been suggested, with reason, that this article was a work of fiction, that the physician did not follow a number of steps he would have if indeed he intended to administer a lethal injection. It is now generally agreed that the article was written to encourage debate within the medical profession. The response to the article, as charted through letters to the editor, was four to one against the action described, and three to one against publication of the piece. However, a number of physicians who did respond pointed out that the situation in which Debbie was seen was unconscionable.

Physicians of all specialties and levels of training who see dying patients in pain and distressed patients deprived of adequate comfort despite "supportive" or "keep comfortable" orders should speak up.

Patients like Debbie do not need to be killed by their physicians to be relieved of their shortness of breath. . . . It is tragic when people are left with severe shortness of breath due to their lung cancer [as] narcotics are immensely helpful for this. . . . People can be made quite comfortable, and nature can still take its course. . . . Shortness of breath, like pain, is a complex symptom. It relates not only to the degree of disease but also to the patient's sense of isolation, loneliness, hopelessness, family stress, and spiritual concerns. A multidisciplinary approach to a patient's symptoms is much more effective than the simple prescription of a medicine.

One letter received was written by a spokesman for the Hemlock Society, an organization which lobbies for the legalization of active euthanasia, but that criticized the action.

We condemn the Debbie case as both illegal and unethical, but by present law and ethics and by the law we hope to achieve in the near future. The Hemlock Society firmly believes in legalized physician aid-in-dying only when it conforms to the following requirements:

1. There must be adequate legal documentation that the euthanasia was requested by the patient well in advance of its occurring.

2. The physician who aids the patient in dying must have known the patient and must have been fully aware of his/her medical history and desire for aid-in-dying in the event of terminal illness.

3. The physician must have a second opinion from another qualified physician that affirms that the patient's condition is indeed terminal.

4. The rights of physicians who cannot in good conscience perform aid-in-dying are to be fully respected, providing they in no way obstruct the practice of physicians who in good conscience give such aid.

After the publication of "It's Over, Debbie," the editors of the journal received a torrent of mail on the subject from ordinary citizens as well. "It may become one of the most predominant medical and ethical debates for the rest of the century," wrote Dr. George D. Lundberg, the journal's editor. He went on to quote letters from the public expressing more tolerance of active euthanasia than the medical community had.

• "Doctors are supposed to alleviate suffering, not prolong suffering and dying."

• "Let's have less profiteering from prolonging dying."

• "In the terminally ill person . . . 'mercy killing' is a part of the treatment."

• "I applaud that physician as one caring more about a patient's pain than about cruel, outdated professional ethics and laws."

• "I am eighty-one years old and I have a profound dread of becoming a vegetable and a burden."

Dr. Lundberg then identified six types of euthanasia. That taxonomy is included here (in italics) for an examination of the degrees by which a physician may ease the passage by expediting an impending death.

1 *Passive. A physician may choose not to treat acute broncho-pneumonia or sepsis [overwhelming infection, e.g., blood poisoning] in a person with Alzheimer's disease or may not resuscitate a patient with carcinomatosis [diffuse spread of cancer] who has experienced earlier arrest.*

Most physicians perform some type of passive euthanasia. It is part of the old-fashioned *easing the passage.* It is the moment at which a physician does not treat an infection.

———

Often the terminally ill patient is unconscious at this point, so I (Hersh) say to the family, "Your Mom is going to die. Do you want me to treat this infection? I cannot cure the underlying disease."

———

2 *Semipassive. A physician may withhold medical treatment, such as nutrition or fluids, from a person in a coma from post-necrotic cirrhosis [liver failure] and hepatoma [liver cancer] with cerebral metastases [cancer spread to the brain].*

This enters the issue of whether the physician is engaging in ordinary or extraordinary acts. If there is no good long-term outlook, for example, because of substantial brain damage, the physician could conclude that to continue administration of nutrition and fluids constitutes extraordinary action, in which case the Living Will should be honored. However, this is where a division begins to exist among physicians. Some would refuse to discontinue hydration. Withholding antibiotics should not be a problem for these physicians because taking antibiotics is not a natural process. According to some, however, hydration is natural, and it possibly is not acceptable for them to discontinue it.

3 *Semiactive. A physician may disconnect a ventilator from a patient who is in a stable, vegetative state from massive cerebral infarction [stroke] and who has no hope of regaining consciousness.*

This requires an act of commission. There is no difference, according to the President's Commission, but it feels very different to the physician. Withholding is much easier than withdrawing. It is why many physicians do not like to start procedures, although from the ethical, moral, or legal point of view it is the considered opinion that there is no difference.

On the other hand, there *are* treatments that I (Hersh) initiate to prove to me or to a family that it is *not* working. I want the proof that there is no cure. But because I always find it difficult to turn off a respirator, there are times when I might not wish to turn one on. A Living Will or an agent with Durable Power of Attorney for Health Care makes my decision easier. It also makes an action such as withdrawing a respirator less complicated for me as the physician in terms of liability, and it is better for the family in terms of guilt. Without a Living Will or an agent for guidance, the physician is asking, "What would your mother say if she could tell us what she wanted?" Having it in black and white is a strong support for the unfortunate family member who has to say, "Pull the respirator," and is told twenty minutes later, "Your mother is dead." He then has to live with the fact that he "killed" his mother, he gave the order. The same is true for the physician.

---

4 *Accidental ["double effect"]. A physician may administer a narcotic to relieve bone pain in a patient with terminal metastatic breast cancer [cancer that has spread throughout the body] and the narcotic may incidentally depress respiration sufficiently to cause death directly or facilitate the development of fatal bronchopneumonia.*

The use of painkillers—administering increasingly high dosages of narcotics—is probably the most common form of easing the passage. Most physicians have done it with cancer patients: she is in pain, let's increase the dose. In fact she may not be in pain but is able to do nothing more than grunt. It is the equivalent of turning the respirator down little by little until the oxygen flow is incompatible with life. Morphine is a respiratory suppressant, but because the patient is so sedated, there is no sense of a lack of oxygen. The patient dies quietly.

5 *Suicidal. A person with metastatic lung cancer may intentionally overdose on alcohol and barbiturates, causing his or her own death; the drugs may have been provided by a physician.*

In many instances this is physician-assisted suicide. (A recent survey by *USA Today* indicated that 68 percent of those interviewed believed that a person with a terminal illness should be allowed to commit suicide.) Either it is overt, when the patient has asked for a lethal amount of medication, or it is a covert understanding. The physician prescribes fifty pills but warns the patient that to take more than twenty at one time will cause death. A physician who does this could put himself in legal jeopardy, but the medical community is more sympathetic than might be expected to a request for a big dosage. What physicians do not want to see are a lot of showmen like Dr. Kevorkian who get up on a pedestal and say, "Look what I've done." (Most of the public, however, supports physician-assisted suicide in cases like this.)

An overdose of pills is probably the most frequent way in which people try to commit suicide, and the Hemlock Society's book *Let Me Die Before I Wake*, essentially a how-to tract—emphasizes this alternative. The problem is that it may not work and instead may result in brain damage. It is unreliable because of variable absorption from the intestinal tract, improper dosage, and threat of vomiting. If someone is serious about dying, the intravenous route is much better and possibly more dignified. However, because the signs of a massive dosage of morphine are so overt, the drug is often administered by a physician gradually over a couple of days, during which the patient is comfortably sedated.

6 *Active. A physician may administer a large, surely fatal overdose of morphine or potassium to a patient with the acquired immunodeficiency syndrome [AIDS] who has widespread Kaposi's sarcoma,* Pneumocystis carinii *pneumonia, or the dementia of cerebral toxoplasmosis [terminal events in AIDS].*

——————

This is murder under current law, but in the course of working on this book, I (Hersh) have heard all sorts of stories from colleagues. One physician could not stand what was happening with his patient anymore, took some potassium chloride— which is essentially untraceable—and administered an injection. The important difference between this and the "Debbie" case is that the physician in this instance knew his patient, had a copy of her Living Will, and had discussed this option in a prior meeting with the family. Although the physician still could be prosecuted, his active participation was not reported, because there was physician-patient-family agreement on easing the passage.

——————

A "natural death act" authorizing active euthanasia will be considered in 1991 by the Washington and Oregon legislatures and in 1992, through a referendum, by the citizens of California. If the act passes, it is likely that other states and the medical profession itself will begin to consider the issue. These state initiatives remove criminal penalties from a physician who honors the request of a terminally ill patient to help him or her die. A number of pharmaceutical alternatives, all of which cause death within a few seconds, are available to physicians.

CHAPTER NINE

Easing the Passage: Hospice

It is possible to make all of the arrangements to ease the passage by oneself, and it is *essential* that a number of steps be completed individually. There is, however, an organization created specifically to help dying patients and their families. It is called Hospice.

The tragic story of Irma (see chapter 4) would have been very different had Hospice been involved. (Irma's case took place in 1975, and a number of other mechanisms and understandings for easing the passage are now available. Nonetheless, in some form Irma's story is still being played out every day, through ignorance of other options.) The critical words in Irma's husband's account are *there are to be no heroic measures*. With the steps outlined in this book, forced artificial nutrition could have been withdrawn, a chemical restraint (that is, a tranquilizer) could have been substituted for physical restraints (that is, binding Irma's hands to the rails), and pneumonia would have ended her life without pain in less than forty-eight hours. The physicians, nurses, and practitioners of Hospice know and practice this. It is the case of ordinary versus extraordinary—or heroic—procedures that only prolong the process of dying.

Hospice defines itself as follows:

> A coordinated program of palliative [for example, pain control] and supportive services provided in both home and inpatient settings which provides for physical, psychological,

social, and spiritual care for dying persons and their families. Services are provided by a medically directed interdisciplinary team of professionals and volunteers. Hospice provides support and care for persons in the last phases of incurable disease so that they may live as fully and comfortably as possible. Hospice recognizes dying as part of the normal process of living and focuses on maintaining the quality of remaining life. Hospice affirms life and neither hastens nor postpones death.

One of the most interesting references to Hospice appears in John Naisbitt's best-selling book, *Megatrends*. In determining the controlling trends in our society, Naisbitt observed that every new development of high technology is followed by a balancing development of "high touch." Our humanism, he argues, demands this. With the advances in medical technology—an impersonal, scientific enterprise—the birth of Hospice, a personal, nontechnological alternative form of medical care was to be expected.

Before explaining specifically what Hospice does, and how to take advantage of its service, an important cautionary note must be interjected. Not all Hospices are the same; important qualitative differences exist between various categories of Hospice.

Most unfortunately, the National Hospice Organization (NHO) has lost control over the use of the name *hospice*. NHO is an organization that maintains a directory of local Hospices across the United States. It also promulgates a list of standards for local Hospices that are members of the umbrella organization.

This is contrary to limitations on use of the word *hospital*, for example. The law protects against anyone's setting up a facility and calling it a hospital. Although the origins of the word *hospice* have the same Latin root as the word *hospital*, and its general meaning in English is similar, it is not protected. It is important to understand this and to be able to identify whether a Hospice is certified by the NHO and is medically certified for Medicare reimbursement.

At the most primitive, and possibly most anachronistic level, a Hospice is nothing more than a building that has been purchased and so named. Because *hospice* has a worthy connotation, it is easy to raise money for any venture with that word in it. Recently, some AIDS groups have purchased nursing homes or empty mansions and called them Hospices. While these places may be doing good work, they may not be accredited by NHO because they do not follow the basic standards and principles established by that organization.

There are also Hospices run by members of the National Association for Home Care (NAHC) under its subunit called the Hospice Foundation of America, which claims to represent more Hospices than any group in this country. NAHC uses the term *"Hospice"* to describe a form of home care used by home health agencies. According to Ira Bates, former vice president of Programs/Services for the NHO,

> The Hospice Foundation of America is the tail of a very large dog: home care. The Visiting Nurse Associations are part of this, and do good work. Other home care agencies are downright sleazy, recruiting aides right off the street. Many have a terrible reputation. Furthermore, if "hospice" is defined as care of dying people, then every hospital in America is a Hospice; every nursing home is a Hospice; every home health agency is a Hospice. Because people are dying in all these situations, what is *not* a Hospice?
>
> The major difference that distinguishes NHO and its affiliate Hospices is that our interest is Hospice *exclusively*. Our definition of a Hospice is an alternative system of health care for the terminally ill, an alternative to traditional care treatment. Our goal is to keep a patient at home, or in a nursing home if that *is* their home, and to operate from the principle that there is no need to move them back to a hospital. This needs to be negotiated with the patient and family in terms of their desires and wishes. They may not be ready for Hospice, because being ready to die implies an acceptance of the condition of terminal illness.

The NHO makes a distinction between a terminal disease— a disease which ultimately leads to death—something we will all encounter at some point, and a terminal illness, which is a physician's prognosis of impending death. The NHO adds a prognosis of death within six months to its working definition of eligibility.

Thus there is some consistency among regional Hospices that are members of NHO. There is another confusion, however. Even the NHO-member Hospices fall into two categories: those that provide managed medical supervision and those that are principally supportive in a hand-holding role.

In the Middle Ages, hospices were refuges created by religious orders for pilgrims on perilous journeys to the Holy Land. The metaphorical translation for this, and the origin for the modern-day Hospice in America, comes from the work of Dame Cicely Saunders in England. This saintly woman, who was working in a cancer ward, in the 1960s established a specialized program of palliative medical care for the dying. In England, because of the structure of socialized medicine, the care was provided not at home but in an inpatient facility.

In the early 1960s Dame Saunders came to the United States for a lecture tour, and such was her charisma and her humane understanding of the needs of dying people that "wherever she made a speech there is a Hospice." Partly as a result of that, there remains a significant misconception in this country: that a Hospice is a *place*. A Hospice *can* be a place, but evolution of the movement in the United States has been to meet a different need, which is principally a wish to die at home. One study indicates that 95 percent of this country's population wish to die at home, and the original prototype for Hospice that was in the United States set up on the English model failed because so few people wanted to go there to die.

As individual Hospices staffed by volunteers became established across the states, their initial role was largely that of psychological and social support. They were a friend to the dying person, but they could do little for pain. Nurses and physicians who were volunteers in this effort realized over time that they could make a greater contribution to terminally ill patients if they could provide medical service as well. In a further evolution it became obvious that there should be an umbrella organization that could monitor and assist the network of independent Hospices. The NHO, a nonprofit, tax-exempt entity governed by a board of directors drawn from regional Hospices, is the result.

The NHO has a set of twenty-five standards for Hospice care. A synthesis of the most significant is given here because they reveal the intent and scope of Hospice as an agent in easing the passage. Any organization that becomes a member of NHO is asked to self-comply with these standards.

1 The Hospice program must establish and maintain appropriate policies, procedures, and reporting, to ensure that the Hospice is accountable to the community.

2 The program must comply with applicable local, state, and federal laws and regulations governing the organization and delivery of health care.

3 Access to Hospice medical and nursing services is to be available on a twenty-four-hour basis, seven days a week.

4 Admission criteria must reflect the patient/family's desire and need for Hospice care. To the maximum extent possible, the Hospice will admit patients regardless of their diagnosis or ability to pay for services.

5 Access to a Hospice inpatient facility is available either directly by the Hospice or through contract or arrangement with such a facility. However, any inpatient facility must comply with all applicable regulations. All Hospice inpatient personnel must be trained in the provision of Hospice inter-disciplinary team care.

6 The patient/family is the unit of care in Hospice and support is provided to both the patient and the family. Hospice acknowledges that each patient/family has its own values and beliefs and is respectful of them. Hospice encourages patient/family participation in the development of the interdisciplinary team plan of care.

7 The Hospice program seeks to identify, teach, coordinate, and supervise those persons acting as primary care givers for the patient. If a primary care person is not available, the Hospice program seeks to develop a substitute network.

8 The goal of all intervention is to maximize the quality of remaining life through the provision of palliative therapies that control symptoms including the optimal relief of pain and minimization of the side effects of intervention.

9 The Hospice program has an organized training program and procedures for the selection, supervision, and continuing evaluation of volunteers, and it offers volunteer support to each patient/family admitted to its program of care.

10 The Hospice program care is provided by an interdisciplinary team that includes at least the following members: patient and patient's family, physician, nurse, social worker, volunteer, and clergy.

11 The Hospice program maintains accurate, current, integrated clinical records, and provides assurances for the confidentiality of these records. These clinical records must include a signed informed consent form completed by the patient or a designated representative. This form must inform the patient/family of the palliative nature of Hospice care; the avoidance, if at all possible, of injections, diagnostic testing, and curative measures; and the nonuse of heroic measures to prolong the dying process, consistent with the patient/family wishes.

12 The Hospice program provides bereavement services to the surviving family members for at least one year after the death of the patient.

13 The Hospice program has quality assurance and utilization review programs.

These standards were prepared after the 1983 legislation that authorized qualified Hospice expenses to be reimbursed by Medicare and Medicaid. (It is significant that Hospice benefits under Medicare, a new federal expense, were advocated by President Reagan's notorious budget cutter, David Stockman.) Nonetheless, there are Hospice programs included in the NHO roster that have not yet taken the individual steps for accreditation by state regulatory agencies that lead to Medicare reimbursement. The NHO estimates that by 1993 75 percent of the Hospices in this country will be Medicare-certified. (A list of states and their current Hospice-accredited status is listed in "Hospice Services by State," page 151.) Hospices in Maine are the most glaring example of failure to obtain Medicare reimbursement certification. Only one of the eleven regional Hospices in that state has established itself to qualify. The difference between Medicare accreditation and nonaccreditation is made clear in the following fictional, but typical, case.

THE STORY OF MR. SMITH

Mr. Smith is eighty-seven years old. He has suffered two heart attacks and three moderate strokes. In each case he was admitted to the hospital and subsequently released. He has executed a Living Will and a Durable Power of Attorney for Health Care and has strongly expressed his wish to die at home. Mr. Smith has congestive heart failure, and his personal physician has indicated that he probably will die within six months.

Mr. Smith contacts the local Hospice program, which is Medicare-certified. A Hospice representative meets with him and with his next of kin. The nature of this alternative health care procedure is explained—namely, that the goal is maximum relief from pain, discomfort, and stress. A move toward recognition that the illness is terminal is a key point in this dialogue. Mr. Smith agrees and signs a statement of informed consent to this program. Hospice then establishes a plan with the primary care giver and has a conference with Mr. Smith's personal physician. It is understood that if Mr. Smith's heart stops, he will not be resuscitated. The do-not-resuscitate (DNR) order is then sent to the local ambulance/emergency health organization, the hospital, and any other appropriate group. The standard 911 phone number for emergency is replaced by a special Hospice exchange.

Because a heart attack and pneumonia and other attendant diseases can be painful, procedures for home administration of pain control, without hospital admission, is prepared. The necessary drugs and medical equipment for home care are procured. If in the opinion of Hospice an inpatient facility is necessary during the course of the illness for some reason, Mr. Smith will be admitted to a hospital with a Hospice agreement, for the minimal possible stay. There he will be attended to by the same team who has been caring for his well-being at home. All of this will be covered by Medicare. As at home, a do-not-resuscitate order will be in place, and there will be no bloodletting or diagnostic procedures. It is very controlled; the Hospice representative advises the hospital staff: "You will follow our plan." As is discussed elsewhere in this book, however, a staff physician may have a different set of beliefs or values and may wish to institute more aggressive procedures. At that point, the Hospice representative will explain that Mr. Smith has indicated he does not want that done. If the physician persists, he will be told that Hospice will help the patient/family sue the physician, that there is a body of law to support such a suit, and that the hospital, a Hospice affiliate, will not support the physician in this.

Such a Hospice program for Mr. Smith is defined as *managed* care. If the Hospice has not completed the Medicare accreditation process, it may still meet the other criteria of NHO. For Mr. Smith, however, there will be a big difference. In an emergency someone will have to call 911, and hospital admission will be through the emergency department. The most the local Hospice can do is provide patient support, which is more a function of hand-holding: bringing flowers, driving the patient to an appointment, and the like. Such functions have a place, and were the original focus of Hospice when it was established in the United States, but today they represent the smaller part of an available benefit.

Forty-two state Hospice organizations and some fifteen hundred local Hospice programs are now affiliated with NHO. In 1989, they worked with more than 200,000 dying patients and their families, and the number is growing at an annual rate of almost 10 percent. Most of this took place in an *in-home* setting. Hospices are increasingly Medicare-accredited, making them eligible for reimbursement. Furthermore, in a survey of the nation's fourteen hundred largest companies, two of three provide a Hospice benefit in their group health coverage. The reasoning behind this coverage is obvious, if monetary: it costs considerably less to care for a patient at home than in a hospital.

Summarizing the growth and availability of Hospice as an alternative program of health care, Ira Bates said that the 1970s was a decade when Hospices began to work with dying patients at home and the 1980s was a period in which they solidified their contracts with hospitals and obtained legislative ability for health insurance reimbursement to their patients. For the 1990s, in addition to an increased role in both these areas, NHO will be becoming more active in working with terminal patients in nursing homes. According to Bates,

> The single consistent indicator of satisfaction in a nursing home is public access. When Hospice is caring for a patient, there is a great deal of traffic to that bedside, and before long the patients in other beds will be aware of what our program of managed care means, and they will be asking for our help as well. As for the administrators of these nursing homes, they will realize that our presence not only helps them with dying patients, but provides a financial base. Over time, nursing homes—which in America are the *last* places a person wants to go and be "warehoused"—will be transformed.

113

CHAPTER TEN

Easing the Passage: Control of Pain

Because the greatest fear associated with the thought of death is pain, the subject is being treated as a separate chapter. Surveys have shown that people associate unrelieved physical pain with terminal illness, and there is justification for this. Medical studies have indicated that perhaps *as little as 10 percent and certainly less than 50 percent of the population obtain effective relief from pain.*

Pain is unnecessary, because pain can be controlled. There is an arsenal of pharmaceutical remedies for pain. In addition, hypnosis, biofeedback techniques, and other forms of conditioning have proved effective as ancillary treatments.

Why, then, is pain a problem in the 1990s? The answer is fourfold.

1 Many physicians are not up to date in their knowledge of existing pain remedies. "Expertise in pharmacologic approaches alone could probably provide relief for at least 70 percent of cancer patients with pain. The combination of several modalities can help most of the other 30 percent," wrote Russell K. Portenoy.

2 When it *is* given, medication is often administered inadequately. Two physicians, Edward T. Creagan and John M. Wilkinson, writing in *American Family Physician*, stated: "Many patients suffer needlessly because they are given analgesic in doses that are too low or are spaced too far apart." "It is customary to undertreat all pain," wrote C. Stratton

Hill, director of pain service at M. D. Anderson Cancer Center in Houston.

3 Patients are fearful of an addiction. Indeed the very word *drugs* carries a frightening connotation for many.

4 For a similar reason physicians themselves are uneasy with dispensing narcotics. Another physician, John Morgan, has argued that physicians have "developed an opiophobia that prevents prescribing opiates in adequate doses. This phobia is like all others—not subject to rational correction."

By understanding the basis for these obstacles and their remedy, a reader can take steps to guarantee that pain will not be a part of his or her death.

Palliation of pain has no special niche in medicine, even though the medications and ways to administer them are constantly changing. Even oncologists, who are normally confronted with pain in their patients, more often than not fail to use the most effective regimen of pain medication. It may be difficult, however, for the layperson to confront the physician on this subject, let alone be able to participate in a technical discussion of options. Hospice, however, knows this subject thoroughly. Control of pain is its single most important function, as self-defined. Even Hospice programs that are not certified for Medicare reimbursement often can informally recommend physicians in the community who can provide helpful consultation on control of pain.

Pain is more easily prevented than halted. For a terminally ill patient the focus should be changed from curing the illness to preventing pain. If, then, the goal is to relieve pain absolutely, analgesics should be administered *regularly*. Physicians who prescribe pain medication when the patient requests it have created a situation in which pain is allowed to occur before it is dealt with. Not only does this create *unnecessary* pain, it places a burden on the patient. For many individuals it is a debasing situation to have to beg for pain relief, and medically it is unconscionable. A clear understanding about pain prevention should exist among patient, physician, and family from the time of diagnosis of a terminal condition.

The concern that a drug may be addictive is irrelevant and meaningless for a dying patient. Even in patients who have defied the prognosis and recovered, a regimen of pain-relieving narcotics has not led to an addiction.

In the case of cancer patients for whom the likelihood of pain is highest, morphine is a drug of choice. In England, the Brompton cocktail was created for cancer patients. It consists of heroin, morphine, cocaine, and flavorings. In this country, because heroin cannot be legally administered, the formula is usually morphine, ethanol, cocaine, and flavorings. Another common drug in pain control is methadone.

There is a confusion, however, among both medical personnel and laypeople on the effects of narcotics. The words *dependence* and *addiction* are often used synonymously but in fact describe different things. A third word is also relevant: *tolerance.* Tolerance is defined medically as a state in which a current dose of medication is no longer effective and an increased amount is required to obtain the previous effect. Over time, tolerance to a drug such as morphine increases, meaning that the dosage must be increased. This has nothing to do with addiction or dependence. Dependence defines only the patient's reliance on the medication to prevent pain. Dependence is a biological reaction: the body relies on the medication for pain relief. People with a disease that produces pain are dependent on a drug to eliminate the pain. Addiction, on the other hand, is not a medical condition so much as a psychological one, a lifestyle centered on obtaining and using drugs. A patient with chronic pain becomes dependent on a drug to alleviate the condition and over time experiences a higher tolerance. That is, he or she requires more of the drug for effective pain control. This dependence, however, is physical and only rarely leads to a psychological dependence—addiction. Abuse and withdrawal, symptoms associated with addiction, are a remote risk for a patient taking medication for pain, even when the dosage is necessarily high. Writing in *American Family Physician*, Creagan and Wilkinson added: "While longterm use of narcotic analgesics in patients with severe cancer pain will produce tolerance and physical dependence, addiction is rare. The misplaced fear of drug addiction in terminally ill patients deprives these patients of adequate pain control *and a peaceful death*" (emphasis added). One of the dangers of narcotics, highly publicized in this country's fight against the illegal use of drugs, is that they provide a period of euphoria. This may be true in drug abusers, but it is unlikely in the administration of narcotics to eliminate pain in a terminally ill patient. If, however, it does produce a sense of euphoria, is that a sin in this situation? The Brompton Hospital's formula of heroin, morphine, and cocaine has as its purpose a pain-free, tranquil, yet alert time in the final days of life.

To ease the passage, then, the patient, physician, family, and other care givers must be clear on establishing a program that *prevents pain*, and the decisions for such a schedule of medication should not be tainted by any uneasiness about likelihood of addiction. When the remedy for pain is readily available in a variety of pharmaceutical prescriptions, who would want to be part of the 50 to 90 percent of today's patients who unnecessarily receive inadequate relief from pain? Just as the execution of a Living Will can bypass many of the obstacles to easing the passage, insistence on adequate pain prevention will prevent the single largest perceived obstacle to a tranquil death.

Easing the Passage is not intended to make its readers experts in pain medication. To be able to discuss this important aspect of patient care with a physician, however, a few general facts about pain medication should be understood.

First, as already noted, it is much easier to prevent pain than to relieve it. Thus a scheduled regimen that prevents pain is far preferable to doses given on patient request. The scheduled regimen should be of sufficient amount and frequency to prevent pain in the first place. There is a secondary medical reason for this principle. On-request dosing can cause radical fluctuations in plasma levels with the result that the patient bounces between periods of pain and toxicity, which in turn means that the patient experiences such a dramatic rush of relief that dependency is exacerbated rather than minimized. Pain also has other side effects—including insomnia, loss of appetite, and nausea—that are eliminated if pain is prevented.

Second, administration of pain medication at home is now practical. In general, pain medication can be delivered by five routes: intravenously (into a vein), intramuscularly (into a muscle), subcutaneously (under the skin), orally, or by means of a rectal suppository. The last three vehicles are easily accomplished at home, and recent developments have refined these applications. The oral route is the simplest and is possible in most patients. Until fairly recently, morphine, for example, was far more effective by intravenous delivery, which was best accomplished at an inpatient facility; it was significantly less effective taken orally. Morphine sulfate tablets that provide prolonged pain control are now available, however, and can be prescribed in a sustained-release form (MS Contin, for example). There has also been a breakthrough in the non-oral administration of morphine. A physician can prescribe morphine and other narcotics to be administered under the skin by a small pump. The dosage and frequency is preset by the physician, although in the newer pumps some options can be programmed so the patient can call up a supplemental dose if there is a surge of pain. These pumps deliver the drug through a tiny needle placed under the skin that is easily relocated every week or so by that patient or a care giver.

Third, tolerance to a narcotic is inevitable, meaning that the amount required is going to increase. Family and care givers must not try to moderate the dosage because of a fear that they are encouraging a harmful dependence. In *Scientific American Medicine*, N. H. Cassem wrote: "Tolerance is inevitable and should be expected. In two weeks, the patient on a regular regimen will require at least 50 percent more of the narcotic. However, the increase is much more rapid in the first few weeks of therapy than it is thereafter."

Fourth, psychological elements can add to pain and make it more difficult to treat. Anxiety and depression become part of a self-fulfilling prophecy: fearing pain, the patient creates a lower threshold for pain, making it more difficult to eliminate. By initiating scheduled pain medication at the early stages of a terminal illness, these anxieties can largely be laid to rest.

Fifth, several distinct groups of chemicals are used in pain therapy. The more general classes of pharmaceutical pain controls are listed in the Glossary.

Sixth, even if a patient is unable to communicate, especially in the case of a terminal cancer, *it is still highly unlikely that pain has abated*. Therefore, there should be no lessening of dosage and frequency; in fact, the opposite may be required. That the dying patient is easing more and more into a state of unconsciousness is not due to the level of medication but rather to the body's surrendering life to the disease. To quote Drs. Creagan and Wilkinson again, "Inadequate amounts of narcotic in the terminal stages only increase patient discomfort and agitation, causing unnecessary distress for patients, and their families."

Seventh, because narcotics and other pain medication can cause side effects, a physician may be reluctant to increase dosages. Medical studies have shown, however, that the increasing tolerance to the medication is normally accompanied by a similar tolerance to adverse side effects.

Finally, as has been stressed throughout this book, medicine has the ability to prolong life considerably. It should be incumbent on care givers to guarantee that the days a person lives with a terminal illness be totally pain-free. If there is any failure in this area, the passage has not been eased, the family has not been able to say farewell in a tranquil and dignified environment, and the principle of "First, do no harm" has been violated.

CHAPTER ELEVEN

Easing the Passage:
Comfort

*C*omfort is such a nice word and such a simple concept. Somehow the word itself is comforting. Comfort for a terminally ill patient is a form of care that is so easily provided; it may be something as simple as rearranging a pillow. Unfortunately, because professionals—physicians and nurses—are primarily concerned with *medical* treatment, the attention to comfort is often secondary and sometimes ignored. A dying person has a basic right to experience comfort, and caretakers have a basic obligation to provide it. Even in the context of a hospital death, however, this is not guaranteed.

More than any discussion or contemplation of death and of easing the passage, consideration of measures to achieve comfort may trigger a defense mechanism of avoidance. People can discuss withdrawal of artificial life-support systems more easily than treatment of constipation and bedsores. This is probably because we can stay at a level of abstraction on the former, but the latter has a level of specificity that can make us squeamish. Yet the matter of comfort is as important as pain control in easing the passage. In earlier times, when people spent their dying days at home, providing comfort would have been second nature to those around them. In today's world we must relearn this form of care. Because it is not a priority for the medical specialist, we need to oversee it as family and friends in the same way we would want someone to care for our own needs. Fortunately Hospice, visiting nurse associations, and other groups are well-trained in this area and can assist.

THE STORY OF MISS SCHWARTZ

Miss Schwartz is ninety-nine years old. She is brought to the emergency department with a massive heart attack. The resident on duty does not expect her to survive. Miss Schwartz beats the odds, however. Two days later she has a small stroke. Although conscious, she is not able to move easily and her speech is slurred. Her biggest discomfort is her mouth. When the physician makes his rounds she tells him that her mouth is dry and has a terrible taste. He responds, "I am not a dentist." Whether or not he intended the remark to be funny, he has just ignored an easily corrected part of his patient's comfort.

As in the chapter on pain, readers cannot become experts on providing comfort—which sometimes requires medication—by reading a few pages. But by being sensitive to the more common forms of discomfort, one can seek their redress. The following is a summary of actions that should be *required*. If these comforts are not being provided, they must be demanded of nurses and physicians; they should also be monitored to ensure that they continue.

Simple Physical Comforts

The mouth. Care of the mouth is so basic, but the President's Commission reported that "much *avoidable* distress arises from inattention to the mouth." Why should a clean-tasting mouth, something we routinely accomplish in healthy days, be denied a dying person.

Bedsores. Bedsores are the classic example of an irritant that can be a persistent center of discomfort. It is far easier to prevent—or at least postpone—bedsores than heal them. A patient's position should be changed frequently. Vulnerable parts of the body such as the heels should be protected with padding made for the purpose, and special mattresses (such as the egg-crate variety) used. Skin massage is effective therapy against bedsores, but it must be administered frequently.

Itching. Often a consequence of malignancy, itching can be treated with antihistamines or steroids.

Nausea and vomiting. These are common occurrences in a terminal patient. A number of pharmaceuticals, often in the form of suppositories, are available to treat nausea and vomiting, including tetrahydrocannabinol (THC)—the active ingredient in marijuana. THC was noted for its efficacy by the President's Commission, but it can only be used experimentally.

Gastrointestinal problems. Constipation is normal in a dying patient, and it can go on to cause fever, pain, and other complications. The President's Commission stated: "With assiduous attention and vigorous efforts, nearly all patients can avoid the complications of constipation." The reader should note, however, both the use of the words *assiduous* and *vigorous* and the reality that the problem remains the norm, not the exception. A dying person may also suffer from anorexia (poor appetite) and dysphagia (swallowing difficulties). These are likely to be more upsetting to family than to the patient. "Only rarely should a dying patient be fed by tube or intravenously," cautioned the President's Commission, advice far too frequently ignored.

Fever. Fever can usually be treated with a combination of antipyretics (aspirin or Tylenol), increased fluid intake, and sponge baths.

Environmental Comforts

Environmental comforts can be important to the dignity of a patient. One Hospice worker reported that when visiting a patient the first indicator he gets on the quality of care being given is the presence—or absence—of unnecessary odors such as urine. Inattention to this detail can embarrass a person in his or her final hours of life. Furthermore, it can have a deleterious effect on visiting family and friends even if the patient is no longer conscious. It is a simple matter to mask or eliminate odors. Other physical evidence of the failing body, such as a urine-collecting bag connected to a catheter, can be shielded from sight, although it is one of the details of maintaining patient dignity that is often overlooked. Insofar as possible, all these cosmetic efforts should be directed toward creating an environment of peace and privacy for the person who will only live a little longer.

Psychological Comfort

It is understandable that anxiety and depression should be part of a dying person's outlook. Sometimes these feelings can be caused by a specific frustration. There are cases in which a person has frantically held onto life until seeing a particular person or completing a piece of business, and then died peacefully. It is important for family and care givers to ensure that the dying person has achieved any such desire if possible. If not, persistent anxiety or depression can be treated with mild tranquilizers or antidepressant medications. Drugs of both classes are available that should not cause undesirable excess sedation.

Agonal Symptoms

Agonal symptoms are not associated with "agony" but mean "soon-approaching death." Everyone dies, no matter what the disease, of cardiac arrest and respiratory failure—that is, the heart stops beating and they stop breathing. This may be preceded, however, by hours or even days of difficult breathing. Next to pain the largest fear of death is anticipation of choking or strangling. No symptom is so terrifying as dyspnea (shortness of breath). This can and should be eased by the use of morphine. Pneumonia is often a complication in terminally ill patients. Nicknamed "the old man's friend" it normally causes death within a few days. Whether to treat pneumonia with antibiotics falls into the issue of prolonging life versus prolonging death discussed elsewhere in this book. With the administration of morphine, sedation ensues and the terror and discomfort subside. A slowed respiration then causes an increase of carbon dioxide in the blood, and death follows. Shortness of breath not associated with pneumonia can also be alleviated.

CHAPTER 12

The Family Physician

As one author (Hersh) *is* a family physician, there is a bias in this book toward this branch of medicine. Before World War II, most physicians were not trained in specialties but were general practitioners (GPs), and many of them were accustomed to making house calls. Both authors, and many readers, can remember when the local physician stopped by to swab a strep throat, tie a few stitches in a cut, or salve a burn. After the war, more and more medical students began to specialize and subspecialize, and there was a loss of on-the-job training in the wide range of family practice. GPs tended to be at the bottom end of the class, like washouts in landscape architecture who become gardeners.

Medical education is taught today by specialists, and the family practitioner, who by definition engages in the breadth of medicine, is somehow foreign and threatening. Specialists are uncomfortable with the family practitioner's equal ease with children, adults, and the elderly. The trend today in medical school and residency is to select a narrow area and be the best in that specialty. Recognition is given for achieving that goal, so how is the specialist teacher to evaluate the student whose specialty is generality?

Family practice *is* a specialty in generality. And today, in a reversal of the trend, it is again becoming a more powerful branch of medicine; sixty-five thousand physicians are currently members of the American Academy of Family Physicians.

In addition to the academy, a professional association, there is an accrediting organization, the American Board of Family Practice. Family practice has been recognized by the American Medical Association as medicine's twentieth specialty, and its physicians are trained in a formal post-medical school three-year residency program. Nonetheless, the specialty still encounters some obstacles within medical practice. Some hospitals, for example, do not allow a family practitioner to practice obstetrics or to admit a patient to an intensive care unit without consultation. These are political barriers for a family physician: they are not based on capability and are not relevant to a physician-patient relationship, especially in the case of easing the passage.

There is a quality of holism in family practice. Instead of looking at a person as a diseased organ, the individual is seen as a whole person and in the broader context of how he or she fits into the family and community; the patient is even viewed metaphysically in terms of his or her relationship to the universe. A patient under the care of a family physician is less likely to be bounced from a referral physician to the next specialist as symptoms develop in various organs. And when a family physician does bring in a consultant, it is less a passing of the patient out of their care than a monitored transfer into the hands of a specialist for specific medical management advice.

Because of this cradle-to-the-grave orientation, a family physician ordinarily is better equipped to help a family at the time of easing the passage and is less likely to abandon the patient to treatment by specialists. (For those considering a family practitioner for their physician, many hospitals maintain a list. Readers can also write to the American Academy of Family Physicians, 8880 Ward Parkway, Kansas City, MO 64114, which maintains a directory by zip code.)

No physician, even one in family practice, is enthusiastic about house calls. (The only exception to this are the few

physicians who specialize in home health services.) How does
one encourage a physician to make a house call? A distinction
should be made here between care of a terminally ill patient
in a home setting and a request to be seen at home for reasons
of patient convenience. In the case of the latter there is a bona
fide reason for a physician to resist this.

———

My (Hersh's) rule of thumb is: no emergency home visits. I
will schedule home visits for homebound patients, as I am
able, when significantly more effort is involved for the patient to get to my office than for me to get to him or her.
Home care is more labor intensive and disruptive to practice for a physician, and the hospital or office is much easier. I do not bill for the time surrounding a home visit that
does not involve patient care. However, a family practitioner will likely have an orientation toward home visits in
the first place. He or she has, in addition, eyes and ears out
in the community: visiting nurses, home attendants, Hospice workers, and the like. I have a lot of homebound patients, but, I do not frequently make house calls because I
can do 80 percent of the assessment on the phone. I can order blood to be drawn and then, in my office, evaluate the
results that come back from the lab. I can advise ancillary
help, family members, and attendants.

———

Emergency or urgent home visits may not be practical for a
physician, who cannot disrupt a day of appointments with
other patients. Furthermore, by definition, in these situations
the patient should be transported to the emergency department, unless a Hospice program is in place.

Insurance companies are gradually acknowledging that
home care is less expensive, and the trend to coverage is building. Various kinds of home care have been developed: durable

medical equipment, home respiratory therapy, even pain management through subcutaneous infusion. The family practitioner is likely to be familiar with all of this and to be able to offer it to his or her patients.

CHAPTER THIRTEEN

The Human Part

This book began with the argument that easing the passage required, first, an acknowledgment of mortality. Everything that has followed flows from that critical, primary understanding. We have written of the paperwork that will set in motion an eased passage at some future date. And we have explained the steps within medicine that can be taken to ease the passage for a dying person. By and large, all of these are self-contained and straightforward.

Acknowledgment of mortality need not be debilitating. Benjamin Franklin, albeit something of a humorist, wrote the words for his gravestone ahead of time:

> *The Body of*
> *B Franklin Printer*
> *(Like the Cover of an Old Book*
> *Its Contents torn out*
> *And stript of its Lettering and Gilding)*
> *Lies here, Food for Worms.*
> *But the Work shall not be lost;*
> *For it will, (as he believ'd) appear*
> *once more,*
> *In a new and more elegant Edition*
> *Revised and Corrected*
> *By the Author*

And then there are the poets. Long fascinated with the topic of death, they have filled volumes. The great Indian poet Rabindranath Tagore is often quoted in books about death. Here is one brief thought of his:

129

*When I go from hence let this be my parting word, that
what I have seen is unsurpassable.*

*I have tasted of the hidden honey of this lotus that
expands on the ocean of light, and thus am I blessed—
let this be my parting word.*

*In this playhouse of infinite forms I have had my play
and here have I caught sight of him that is formless.*

*My whole body and my limbs have thrilled with his touch
who is beyond touch; and if the end comes here, let it come—
let this be my parting word.*

Unique in literary expression about death is the tradition
in Japan of death poems. These were traditionally written at
the very moment of death. The Japanese have prescribed and
formal guidelines for personal expression, but these final
statements were meant to be the opportunity of free thought.
They are invariably philosophical, and written in haiku—a
cryptic seventeen-syllable poem. A few examples:

*Leaves never fall
in vain—from all around
bells tolling.*

*I lift my pillow
closer to the
full moon.*

*Autumn gust:
I have no further business
in this world.*

*Lotus seeds in ten
directions jumping
playfully.*

130

What matter if I live on—
a tortoise lives
a hundred times as long.

From one basin
to another—
stuff and nonsense.

A parting word?
The melting snow
is odorless.

Farewell—and though
there be no budding
in the spring, no
autumn withering
—all is well.

The snow of yesterday
that fell like cherry petals
is water once again.

Morning glory
even though you wither
dawn will break anew.

Kübler-Ross's Stages of Death

Like the poets, but in a different way, this book now returns to the arena of the mind. Elisabeth Kübler-Ross made history in the 1960s with her seminar on death and dying. Kübler-Ross was lecturing in psychiatry in Chicago and, partly to make her lectures more interesting for her students, she decided that death was a subject for group focus. To make the topic even more immediate she arranged to interview a sixteen-year-old girl with acute leukemia. It was the beginning of a study that Kübler-Ross would commit the next few years to and that would open a national discussion of death and dying.

It almost did not happen. When Kübler-Ross first went to the Chicago hospital to request permission to talk with dying patients, she stunned the physicians. Not a single one permitted her to talk to a patient. Some said that they would not allow it on principle; others maintained that their patients were too weak for such a conversation.

> These doctors were both very defensive when it came to talking about death and dying and also protective of their patients in order to avoid a traumatic experience.... It suddenly seemed that there were no dying patients in this huge hospital. My phone calls and personal visits to the wards were all in vain. Some physicians said politely that they would think about it, others said they did not wish to expose their patients to such questioning as it might tire them too much. A nurse angrily asked in utter disbelief if I enjoyed telling a twenty-year-old man that he had only a couple of weeks to live!

Kübler-Ross eventually won permission for herself and her students to interview dying patients, and what she discovered was that most of them *wanted* to talk about the fact that they were dying. Based on a large body of these interviews Kübler-Ross constructed a scenario of dying that includes five attitudinal stages.

FIRST STAGE: DENIAL. When first told that his condition is terminal, the patient says it cannot be true: the blood sample or x ray has been switched with someone else's by mistake. The doctor is wrong, get me a new one. Kübler-Ross rationalized that "denial functions as a buffer after unexpected shocking news, allows the patient to collect himself, and with time, mobilize other less radical defenses."

SECOND STAGE: ANGER. Once it is no longer possible to camouflage the reality of an impending death, one rages at the "injustice " of it: why me? Why not so-and-so who is ninety years old, or so-and-so who is good for nothing anyway? Kübler-Ross writes: "This stage of anger is very difficult to cope with from the point of view of family and staff. The reason for this is the fact that the anger is displaced in all directions and projected onto the environment at times almost at random. The doctors are just no good, they don't know what tests to require and what to prescribe."

THIRD STAGE: BARGAINING. This stage typically is a request for a little more time, often made in secret with God—a contract to do something important for someone else that will require just a bit more time.

FOURTH STAGE: DEPRESSION. Kübler-Ross divides this phase into two parts. What she calls "reactive depression" results from knowledge of such things as the tremendous financial drain of medical treatment. "Preparatory depression" results from the realization that life is soon to end.

FIFTH STAGE: ACCEPTANCE. "Acceptance should not be mistaken for a happy stage," says Kübler-Ross. "It is almost void of feelings. It is as if the pain had gone, the struggle is over, and there comes a time for 'the final rest before the long journey' as one patient phrased it."

Life magazine's coverage of Kübler-Ross and the wide publicity given her book no doubt helped many people confront the dying process. It is also true that many specialists on death and dying have disputed her conclusions, especially the construction of the five stages. It makes common sense that denial, anger, bargaining, depression, and acceptance might accompany the terminal phase of life. However, whether any or all of the stages occur for a particular individual, or in this order, is not preordained.

Edwin Schneidman, who also talked with many dying people, wrote in his book *Voices of Death,*

There is not *one* way to die. Each person dies in a notably personal way. In current thanatology there are those—notably Elisabeth Kübler-Ross—who write about a set of five "stages" of dying, experienced in a specified order. My own experiences have led me to radically different conclusions, so that I reject the notion that human beings, as they die, are somehow marched in lock step through a series of stages of the dying process. On the contrary, in working with dying persons, I see a wide panoply of human feelings and emotions, of various human needs, and a broad selection of psychological defenses and maneuvers—a few of these in some people, dozens in others—experienced in an impressive variety of ways.

A Swedish thanatologist also criticized the Kübler-Ross five stages: "This system rests on her impressions and she has not presented a proper study in which they are verified. The eagerness and satisfaction with which this division into five stages has been adopted in many quarters are remarkable."

Avery Wiseman commented on the Kübler-Ross formula: "Schematic stages—denial, anger, bargaining, depression, acceptance—are at best approximations, and at worst, obstacles for individualization."

The psychological issues of impending death are important because whether the Kübler-Ross stages are right or wrong, knowledge of them (and of the broader range of human emotions suggested by others) opens up the nonmedical, nonprocedural aspects of easing the passage. Readers of this book are urged to read at least some of the other works on the subject listed in "Additional Reading." Without duplicating the discussions contained therein, this book concludes with three points that we believe are central in easing the passage.

Dying at Home

As mentioned elsewhere, the great majority—80 or 90 percent—of people want to die at home, and medical and social services exist to assist in this. It requires being prepared physically to face the death of someone close, but it is one of the times when the Golden Rule should become operative: "Do unto others as you would have them do unto you." (For those not prepared for what may be exhausting labor, and some expenses not currently reimbursed by insurance, the choice of a hospital is not necessarily wrong. It does offer the opportunity of quiet time with a relative unencumbered by the logistics of home care.)

Dying at home has advantages. One spends one's last days in familiar surroundings. Because it is home—without the impediments of visiting hours and the confusions of alien loudspeakers and attendants—it is more tranquil. (Very secondarily, it *can* also be significantly less expensive to die at home.)

There are some disadvantages to dying at home. Health insurance, in a policy that does disservice to itself and the people it covers, often does not cover a variety of home expenses. However, a savvy physician will know some ways around this. But physicians do not like having ill patients at home where they often cannot provide as rapid or as effective treatment. For the terminally ill patient, this concern is far less relevant.

A terminally ill bedridden patient requires caretaking assistance. Bathing, feeding, and toilet needs must be attended to. Relatives may not wish to take on that responsibility and may not know how to obtain help. This situation is not bleak, however, because there are organizations designed to help a family with a person who is dying at home (see chapter 9).

A terminally ill bedridden patient may require medication for pain or discomfort. Although improvements have recently been made in home application of medication, some medications must be given by a qualified person. A medically certified Hospice can arrange this.

Lastly, changes in condition—seizures and the agonal symptoms—are alarming to a nonprofessional, and the temptation to call an ambulance may be strong. The reader should refer to chapters 9 and 11.

Dying at home does have an additional component: it is a reversion to an earlier time when death was a known and experienced moment. The passage from life of someone we care about is going to be present and visible. We believe that dying at home generally enlarges the context of life and loving within a family, albeit a traumatic occasion. There is a cliché to the effect that *death is a lonely process*. For those readers helping an aging relative face the news of a terminal diagnosis, it is important to dispel this notion. It is a fallacy. Death is the *only* event in life that every person has in common. We are all part of a fraternity with the same mortality. It is lonely only if we keep death private, lock it away, try to expunge it. If the event of death becomes a point of discourse (which is one of the purposes of this book), it will not be lonely, but rehearsed within the larger stage of experience. The sin of permitting loneliness occurs only because we *allow* it to happen and avoid the bedside during the time of dying. Attending a dying friend may be awkward because it is an unlearned role. It may be emotional because the specter of survival after death, the impending sense of loss, is extremely painful. For the dying, however, that presence can ensure that care givers provide pain-free, dignified, loving, and comfortable final days and hours.

Finally, something can be offered that is even more important: *an image of immortality*.

———

"You were a good father," I (Outerbridge) told my father just before he died. "What I learned from you will be with me always and is already a part of *my* children. And the things that were important to you I will take care of in the future."

———

We cannot know what immortality is in terms of heaven and the spiritual afterlife. However, there is an immortality of high tensile strength that is part of every human life that needs to be understood at these times. The great poet Jorge Luis Borges wrote: "You yourself are the embodied continuance of those who did not live into your time and others will be (and are) your immortality on earth." If the agnostic found no other clue to afterlife than this, it is enough. We are tomorrow's past, but the past informs the present. We do not know the names of the anonymous craftsmen who built Chartres, but they affect our lives. We do know the names of friends and relatives who die, and how we live thereafter is in part their embodied continuance. We have left footprints as indelible as those of the dinosaurs. Some are short prints: Ronald Blythe, writing of the farmers of Akenfield, said that the straight furrows left on a field were not only a signature on the earth, but a signature on life. Larger statements are the lasting gifts of courage, skepticism, grace, vulnerability, and love. Edwin Schneidman wrote that the great fear of death is of something worse than "naughtment." He named it "oblivionated": a final tormenting thought that it will be as if we never existed. This is an unfounded fear. Time can heal sorrow, but time does not erase those imprints upon the community we call friends.

In 1985, I (Outerbridge) published a weekly newspaper in Maine that produced a special supplement called "Death, a Part of Life." It was the most requested publication we ever issued in terms of demand for supplemental copies. According to readers, part of that demand was due to an excerpt from a children's book written by Leo Buscaglia called *The Fall of Freddie the Leaf*. I think the power of the excerpt had nothing to do with children and everything to do with the parable it provided for an adult reader.

> One day a very strange thing happened. The same breezes that, in the past, had made them dance began to push and pull at their stems, almost as if they were angry. This caused some of the leaves to be torn from their branches and swept up in the wind, tossed about and dropped softly to the ground.
> All the leaves became frightened.

"What's happening?" they asked each other in whispers.

"It's what happens in Fall," Daniel told them. "It's time for leaves to change their home. Some people call it to *die*."

"Will we all die?" Freddie asked.

"Yes," Daniel answered. "Everything dies. No matter how big or small, how weak or strong. We first do our job. We experience the sun and the moon, the wind and the rain. We learn to dance and to laugh. Then we die."

"I won't die!" said Freddie with determination. "Will you, Daniel?"

"Yes," answered Daniel, "when it's my time."

"When is that?" asked Freddie.

"No one knows for sure," Daniel responded.

Freddie noticed that the other leaves continued to fall. He thought, "It must be their time." He saw that some of the leaves lashed back at the wind before they fell, others simply let go and dropped quietly.

Soon the tree was almost bare.

"I'm afraid to die," Freddie told Daniel. "I don't know what's down there."

"We all fear what we don't know, Freddie. It's natural," Daniel reassured him. "Yet, you were not afraid when Spring became Summer. You were not afraid when Summer became Fall. They were natural changes. Why should you be afraid of the season of death?"

"Does the tree die, too?" Freddie asked.

"Someday. But there is something stronger than the tree. It is Life. That lasts forever and we are all a part of Life."

"Where will we go when we die?"

"No one knows for sure. That's the great mystery!"

"Will we return in the Spring?"

"We may not, but Life will."

"Then what was the reason for all of this?" Freddie continued to question. "Why were we here at all if we only have to fall and die?"

Daniel answered in his matter-of-fact way, "It's been about the sun and the moon. It's been about happy times together. It's been about the shade, the old people and the children. It's been about colors in Fall. It's been about seasons. Isn't that enough?"

That afternoon, in the golden light of dusk, Daniel let go. He fell effortlessly. He seem to smile peacefully as he fell. "Good-bye for now, Freddie," he said.

Then, Freddie was alone, the only leaf left on his branch.

The first snow fell the following morning. It was soft, white, and gentle; but it was bitter cold. There was hardly any sun that day, and the day was very short. Freddie found himself losing his color, becoming brittle. It was constantly cold and the snow weighed heavily upon him.

At dawn the wind came that took Freddie from his branch. It didn't hurt at all. He felt himself float quietly, gently and softly downward. As he fell, he saw the whole tree for the first time. How strong and firm it was! He was sure that it would live for a long time and he knew that he had been a part of its life and it made him proud.

Freddie landed on a clump of snow. It somehow felt soft and even warm. In this new position he was more comfortable than he had ever been. He closed his eyes and fell asleep. He did not know that Spring would follow Winter and that the snow would melt into water. He did not know that what appeared to be his useless dried self would join with the water and serve to make the tree stronger. Most of all, he did not know that there, asleep in the tree and the ground, were already plans for new leaves in the Spring.

The Beginning.

Commenting on the physicians' refusal to attend her seminar or to let her talk with patients, Elisabeth Kübler-Ross wrote subsequently:

It was obvious that they missed the whole point of the seminar. We certainly did not wish to talk to dying patients during the last days of their lives. . . . How could we ever bring families together in the very last moment? How could we help to alleviate the loneliness and fear of our patients when we were not allowed to see them before they were on their actual death bed? . . . We could not convey to our colleagues that we are all dying—that we all have to face our finiteness long before we are terminally ill. *This is perhaps the greatest lesson we learned from our patients: LIVE, so you do not have to look back and say: "God, how I have wasted my life."*

We cannot know when we will die. It could happen tomorrow, next year, or perhaps not for several decades. If we acknowledge that death can come at *any time,* we can reorganize our priorities so that when that moment comes, the terrible frustration of things not done is not a burden we carry to the grave. The acknowledgment of mortality should eliminate the mistakes we make under the rationale "I'll fix it later." Because death may not be more than one second away for any of us, it behooves us to perfect the relationships we have with others in our lives, to not have to come to the end of the story before Scrooge is transformed. Dealing with death, that is to say, preparing our careful case so it will not catch us unprepared, is something that can be done long ahead. In fact, the person who acknowledges mortality years and decades before the time of dying will have had a lifetime to prepare and will therefore have an easier passage.

Any individual is the sum total of all experiences of a lifetime, the most significant of which are going to be relationships with the few people—family and friends—who are normally described as loved ones. All of that experience passes into history at the moment of death for the individual, but the experiences that were shared with others live on in memory and become the history.

Easing the Passage is principally a book about practicalities. These must be learned to ensure a tranquil death. The time of dying will always be difficult, but if it can be shorn of unnecessary pain and confusion, the purpose of this book will have been served, which we hope will ennoble life.

Glossary

Acts and omissions. Acts involve active medical treatment, including those comfort measures that may even hasten the moment of death. They also include the withdrawal of medical treatment. Omissions involve the withholding of medical treatment by the direction of the patient, by his or her **advance medical directive,** by instructions of his or her designated agent, or under the principle of **beneficence.**

Acute pain. Pain of a sudden and recent onset, usually self-limited (temporary) and correctable with medical therapy.

Addiction. A psychosocial preoccupation with obtaining and using drugs.

Advance medical directive. A document produced by a **competent** individual that is specifically addressed to the person's physician or that appoints a legally designated agent for health care matters. This document specifies the person's desires regarding medical treatment if he or she were ever incompetent and unable to speak for himself or herself.

Alzheimer's disease. Presenile dementia, which is similar to senile dementia (old age loss of memory) but which occurs in the forty- to sixty-year age group. The disease has a relentless and irreversible course, but it may take the patient a few months to four or five years to reach the stage of complete helplessness.

Analgesic. Medication with pain-relieving properties.

Antidepressant. A drug used to relieve symptoms of depression. Some antidepressants are useful as adjuncts in pain control.

Arrhythmia. An irregular heartbeat, either physiological (not unusual or medically significant) or pathological (indicative of a diseased state). Some arrhythmias, such as ventricular fibrillation and asystole, occur during a cardiac arrest and immediately before death.

Asystole. Absence of a heartbeat.

Auscultation. Process of listening for sounds produced in some of the body cavities, especially the heart and abdomen, to detect physical abnormalities.

Autonomy. The concept that holds that a **competent** patient is entitled to decide whether to be a patient and to make important decisions about treatment.

Barbiturates. A group of drugs used to treat anxiety or insomnia. Currently, another drug group, benzodiazepines (see **tranquilizer**) is more commonly used for these indications.

Beneficence. Acting to benefit patients by sustaining life: treating illness. Health care providers are to pursue only treatment that contributes to the well-being of their patients. The principle of beneficence states that the physician has a legal obligation and a moral duty to use only those treatments that would benefit the patient. If a particular medical intervention, such as resuscitation, is not in the patient's best interest, the physician is morally free (and may be morally obligated) to withhold or withdraw medical intervention.

Best interest. If the incompetent patient has never been **competent**, or if the patient was once competent but never expressed wishes about terminal care, it is meaningless to speak of extended **autonomy**. In these cases it is recognized that a surrogate ought to attempt to serve the best interest of the incompetent. The courts do not normally permit **substituted judgment** when there is no information about the patient's preferences. Only the best interest standard may be applied.

Bioethics. A meld of philosophy, law, and medicine that establishes standards of acceptable medical behavior.

Brain death. The strict definition of brain death, normally that of the Harvard Ad Hoc Committee, requires total absence of responsiveness, reflexes, and electroencephalographic activity for a 24-hour period in the absence of certain drugs or other conditions such as extreme cold that could independently affect these parameters. The decision to discontinue a life support system in many cases revolves around a determination of brain viability. The concept of brain death has been accepted by both medicine and law.

Brompton cocktail. A blend of morphine, cocaine, alcohol, and flavorings administered to alleviate pain in dying people. The formula was developed in England, where heroin is also an ingredient.

Bronchopneumonia. An inflammation of the lung caused by various infectious agents, including bacteria and viruses. The elderly, bedridden, and immunocompromised are most susceptible. In bacterial forms of **pneumonia,** mortality is greatly reduced by treatment with antibiotics.

Cardiac care unit (CCU). A section of a hospital devoted exclusively to the treatment of severe heart disease.

Cardiopulmonary arrest. The cessation of breathing and pulse—the traditional understanding of death.

Cardiopulmonary resuscitation (CPR). Technique used when a person's breathing and pulse have stopped. Thus, CPR is literally a means of bringing the dead back to life. Basic CPR (basic lifesaving) is the combination of airway clearance and maintenance, mouth-to-mouth ventilation (breathing), and closed-chest cardiac compression. These techniques are taught to medical personnel, paramedics, and the public. Advanced CPR (advanced cardiac lifesaving) is done by specially trained health professionals. It involves the insertion of artificial airways (for example, **endotracheal tube**) and the use of mechanical breathing by bag or **respirator.** In addition, medications can be given to strengthen or regulate heart functions. When appropriate, electric shock (defibrillation) is used to restore normal heart rhythm. CPR is now the rule rather than the exception, even though CPR used in this manner has a reported failure rate as high as 56 to 97 percent.

Cerebral. Pertaining to the brain.

Cerebral infarction. A localized area of brain destruction (stroke) caused by blockage of blood flow and lack of oxygen carried by the blood vessel.

Chronic congestive heart failure. A condition resulting from the inability of the heart to pump sufficient blood to meet the needs of the body.

Chronic pain. Pain over a long time span, usually of an incurable, underlying cause.

Code blue. Hospital/medical terminology for **cardiopulmonary arrest.** Depending on physician instructions, this will result in either a **no-code** or **full-code** response.

Cognitive death. See **persistent vegetative state.**

Coma. An acute loss of consciousness that usually consists of a sleeplike state from which a person cannot be roused that may be followed by varying degrees of recovery or that may result in severe, chronic, neurological impairment. See also **persistent vegetative state.**

Competent. Capable of making decisions on one's own behalf. *Competency* allows a patient the right to forego treatment even when the medical profession or society would judge the decision and reasons for the decision irrational.

Dependence. A reliance on pain medication, not to be confused with **addiction.**

Dialysis. Mechanical purification of the blood to remove liquid and chemicals that the kidneys would ordinarily remove if they were functioning properly.

Disclosure. Providing adequate and truthful information for **competent** patients or their legally designated agent to make medical decisions.

Do-not-resuscitate (DNR) order. A physician's order, entered into the patient's medical chart, prohibiting **cardiopulmonary resuscitation** in the event that **cardiopulmonary arrest** occurs.

Durable Power of Attorney for Health Care. A legal document that names an agent who will make health decisions on the part of an individual who becomes unable to express wishes for himself or herself.

Electrocardiogram (EKG). A record of electrical activity of the heart. Tracings can be permanently recorded on paper or observed in real time on an oscilloscope screen.

Electroencephalogram (EEG). A recording of the electrical activity of the brain.

Endotracheal tube. A tube inserted by way of the mouth, throat, and larynx (voice-box) and fixed in place in the trachea (windpipe). The tube is used to deliver oxygen to a patient who has inadequate or absent spontaneous breathing. The oxygen is delivered by a **respirator** or by a manually compressed bag.

Euthanasia. 1. A good death: dying easily, quietly, painlessly. 2. The practice of ending of life in case of incurable disease, which can be subdivided into *passive* euthanasia (allowing death to occur) and active *euthanasia* (causing death).

Full code. Hospital/medical terminology for the patient status when full medical response is desired and expected in the event of **cardiopulmonary arrest.** Also used to describe the act of aggressively performing all modalities of **cardiopulmonary resuscitation** on a patient. Thus full code is both a status and an act.

Harvard criteria for the determination of death. See **brain death.**

Hospice. A program of alternative care for terminally ill patients. See chapter 9.

Hyperalimentation. The intravenous delivery of vitamins and life-sustaining nutrients, in addition to water and minerals.

Hypnotic. A drug that creates insensitivity to pain by inhibiting sensory messages to the brain. Hypnotics also cause partial or complete unconsciousness. Hypnotics include sedatives, **analgesics,** anesthetics, and intoxicants.

Informed consent. Common law dictates that before any person may touch another person's body, he or she must have consent to do so. This principle, which is related to the right of privacy and the right to prevent the invasion of privacy, is applicable to the physician-patient relationship since treatment of a patient usually involves touching.

Intensive care unit (ICU). A section of the hospital devoted exclusively to the care of critically ill or injured patients.

Intramuscular administration. Injection of drugs into a muscle by a hypodermic needle.

Intravenous hydration. The delivery, by a catheter placed in a vein, of water and minerals.

Living Will. A document produced by a **competent** individual stating his or her wishes regarding medical care if he or she were to become incompetent and unable to express his or her desires for health care.

Methadone. Synthetic, orally administered **narcotic** with **analgesic** potency. Its effect is approximately equivalent to that of **morphine** but usually with less sedation.

Morphine. (Name from Morpheus, the Greek god of sleep.) A **narcotic** made from the main active chemical found in opium. Widely used as an **analgesic.**

Narcotics. A group of drugs derived from the opium poppy. In moderate doses narcotics depress the central nervous system, thus relieving pain and producing sleep, but in excessive doses they produce unconsciousness, stupor, coma, and possibly death.

Nasogastric tube. A tube that passes into the stomach by way of the nose and esophagus, through which feeding solutions may pass. This route to the stomach can be used when the patient is unable to swallow.

No code. Hospital/medical terminology for a patient with **do-not-resuscitate** status.

Oncologist. A physician who specializes in the medical treatment and diagnosis of malignant tumors (cancer).

Palliative therapy. Treatment that relieves or alleviates pain without curing the patient.

Palpation. Examination of a patient by the use of touch.

Persistent vegetative state. A chronic state of unconsciousness caused by overwhelming damage to the brain. The body continues to awaken and sleep cyclically, but there is no cognitive function or ability to respond in a learned manner to external events or stimuli.

Pneumonia. See **bronchopneumonia.**

Privacy. A constitutional right for U.S. citizens that has been interpreted to include protection against unwanted medical invasion and intervention.

Respirator. A machine that provides prolonged artificial breathing.

Subcutaneous administration. Injection or infusion of drugs beneath the skin through a hypodermic needle.

Substituted judgment. A legal standard in which a patient's surrogate attempts to make the health care decisions that the patient would make if the patient were competent. Substituted judgment is based on a patient's own values as best as can be determined and may differ from **best interest.**

Thanatology. Science or study of death.

Tranquilizer. A drug that acts to reduce mental tension and anxiety, ideally without interfering with normal mental activity. This ideal state is difficult to obtain. The most commonly used medications are benzodiazepines (brand names include Valium, Librium, Serax, Ativan, and Xanax).

Ventilator. See **respirator.**

Ventricular fibrillation. Arrhythmia characterized by uncoordinated contractions of the heart muscle, resulting in no cardiac output.

Useful Organizations

The Society for the Right to Die/Concern for Dying is an amalgamation of two organizations, both of which had a similar purpose. The society maintains up-to-date Living Wills, Durable Powers of Attorney for Health Care, and so forth, for each state. It provides advice to individuals on the laws with respect to patients' rights in particular medical situations and files briefs in court cases concerning the right to die. The society is a nonprofit organization. In addition to keeping its members apprised of particular state regulations, the society publishes a member newsletter (annual membership is $15).

Society for the Right to Die/Concern for Dying
250 W. 57th Street
New York, NY 10107
Telephone: (212) 246-6973

The *National Hospice Organization* (NHO) is a nonprofit organization that acts as an umbrella group for the various state Hospices as well as the fifteen hundred Hospices that meet NHO criteria. It also can indicate which Hospices are certified for Medicare reimbursement.

National Hospice Organization
1901 N. Moore Street
Suite 901
Arlington, VA 22209
Telephone: (703) 243-5900

The Hemlock Society is a nonprofit organization that lobbies for the legalization of active euthanasia. Its self-stated description is an "educational organization [that] supports the option of active voluntary euthanasia (self-deliverance) for the advanced terminally ill mature adult, or the seriously incurably physically ill person." The society has published a number of documents that explain current law and even provide advice on methods of self-deliverance.

The Hemlock Society
P.O. Box 66218
Los Angeles, CA 90066
Telephone: (213) 391-1871

Additional Reading

Kübler-Ross, Elisabeth. *On Death and Dying*. New York: Macmillan, 1969. This book was the first major work on the subject which received widespread attention.

Kübler-Ross, Elisabeth. *Death, the Final Stage of Growth*. New York: Prentice-Hall, 1975. A collection of essays that focus on the "growthful" qualities of dying.

Kushner, Harold. *When Bad Things Happen to Good People*. New York: Schocken Books, 1981. A compassionate look at the question, "Why me?"

President's Commission for the Study of Ethical Problems in Medicine and Biomedical and Behavioral Research. *Deciding to Forego Life-Sustaining Treatment*. Washington, D.C.: U.S. Government Printing Office, 1983. A humane, if technical, examination of health care for the terminally ill. (Out of print, but possibly available in an abridged report from Concern for Dying.)

Thomas, Lewis. *The Lives of a Cell*. New York: Penguin, 1978. A discussion of many aspects of life, including death.

Hospice Services by State

The following breakdown indicates the current number of local Hospice services available in each state and the number that are Medicare-certified for reimbursement.

State	NHO-certified	Medicare-certified	State	NHO-certified	Medicare-certified
Alabama	30	25	Minnesota	65	18
Alaska	8	0	Mississippi	9	4
Arkansas	13	9	Missouri	36	20
Arizona	17	10	Montana	15	6
California	152	56	Nebraska	19	7
Colorado	25	21	Nevada	7	3
Connecticut	29	7	New Hampshire	23	1
Delaware	3	3	New Jersey	39	28
District of Columbia	5	3	New Mexico	11	6
Florida	36	32	New York	68	38
Georgia	32	20	North Carolina	69	49
Hawaii	9	4	North Dakota	8	4
Idaho	14	9	Ohio	70	44
Illinois	71	32	Oklahoma	16	8
Indiana	35	9	Oregon	35	13
Iowa	49	17	Pennsylvania	96	49
Kansas	38	6	Rhode Island	6	4
Kentucky	28	18	South Carolina	17	9
Louisiana	22	16	South Dakota	12	4
Maine	22	1	Tennessee	31	16
Maryland	37	14	Texas	61	41
Massachusetts	44	27			
Michigan	82	32			

Hospice Services by State

State	NHO-certified	Medicare-certified	State	NHO-certified	Medicare-certified
Utah	10	2	West Virginia	15	7
Vermont	14	10	Wisconsin	52	30
Virginia	37	6	Wyoming	7	1
Washington	34	21			

The National Hospice Organization (see Useful Organizations) can direct a reader to a state Hospice association, which can in turn indicate the location of local Hospices.

Index

Index

Easing the passage, 3
EEG (Electroencephalogram),
144
EKG (Electrocardiogram), 144
Elephants, death of, 5
Emanuel, Linda and Ezekiel,
60
Emergency medical care, 127
Endotracheal tube, 144
England:
Hospice movement, 108
pain medication, 116
English, Dr., 46
Environmental comforts, 122–
23
Ethical considerations, 71
acts and omissions, 79–81
euthanasia, 97
guidelines for physicians, 14
Euthanasia, 1, 95–104, 144
Extraordinary treatments, 82–
83, 101

The Fall of Freddie the Leaf,
Buscaglia, 137–39
Families:
and DNR orders, 83–84
and Hospice care, 109–10
and medical decisions, 48–49
Family doctors, old time, 3
Family physicians, 26, 27, 125–
28
Family structures, and death, 9
Fear:
of death, 3, 137
of pain, 119
Feeding devices, artificial, 122
legal considerations, 38–40
Maine legislation, 52
Ferber, Max, 30–32
Fever, 122
Field, George, 54
Forced feeding, 122
Forced treatment, 78–79

Foregoing of life-sustaining
treatment, 71–72, 75–76
Franklin, Benjamin, 129
Full code, 144
Funeral customs, 10–11

Gastrointestinal problems, 122
Generality, specialty in, 125–26
General practitioners (GPs), 125
Goldbeck, Willis, 41
Good death, 1–2
Gray, Jim, 77–78
Grief, 6
Group health insurance, 44–45
Hospice benefits, 113

Handicapped people, treatment
of, 59
Harvard criteria of death, 33–
34
Health care documents, ad-
vance medical instruc-
tions, 47–62
Health care proxies, 54–55
Health maintenance organiza-
tions (HMOs), 44–45
Hemlock Society, 99–100, 147–
48
Let Me Die Before I Wake, 103
Herbert, Clarence, 45
Heroic treatments, 82–83
Hersh, Alan R., medical train-
ing, 26–27
Hill, C. Stratton, 114–15
Hippocratic Oath, 22–25
and euthanasia, 96
HMOs (Health maintenance
organizations), 44–45
Holism, in family practice, 126
Home, death at, 9, 108, 134–36
Home care:
Hospice, 107, 113
insurance and, 41–42
pain medication, 118

Index

Life-prolonging medical treatment, 14
foregoing of, 71–72, 75–76
Life-supports, artificial:
legal considerations, 38–40
Maine legislation, 52
The Lives of a Cell, Thomas, 5
Living Wills, 8, 16, 47–54, 62, 102, 145
and artificial life-supports, 38
hospitals and, 34–36
and persistently vegetative states, 56–57
Loneliness of death, 9, 136
Los Angeles Times, and CPR, 21
Loss, from bereavement, 6
Lou Gehrig's disease, 75
Lundberg, George D., 100–101

Maine:
Hospices, 111
Living Wills, 51–52
Managed care, 112
A Manual of Death Education, Morgan, 25
Marijuana, 122
Medicaid, 42–43
and Hospice, 111
Medical career, choice of, 28–29
Medical profession, and death, 10
Medical schools:
and death, 26–32
and specialization, 125
Medical technology, and dying process, 11
Medical treatment, inappropriate, 17–22
Medicare, 41–44
and Hospice, 111–13
certified Hospice services by state, 151–52

Medication:
home care, 135
methods, 118
Medicine, 25
modern, 7
Megatrends, Naisbitt, 106
Mercy killing. *See* Euthanasia
Metcalf, Peter, *Celebrations of Death*, 10–11
Methadone, 116, 145
Middle Ages, hospices, 108
Miles, Steven, 39
Minors, and wills, 9
Missouri Supreme Court, Cruzan decision, 7, 48
Modern medicine, and maintenance of life, 7
Morgan, Ernest, *A Manual of Death Education*, 25
Morgan, John, 115
Morphine, 103–4, 116, 118, 123–24, 145
Mortality, acknowledgment of, 3, 6–12, 129, 140
Mouth, care of, 121
Moynihan, Patrick, 49
MS Contin, 118
Murder, 79
Murphy, Donald, 20

NAHC (National Association for Home Care), 107
Naisbitt, John, *Megatrends*, 106
Narcotics, 145
euthanasia by, 103
pain control, 115, 116–17
Nasogastric tubes, 145
National Association for Home Care (NAHC), 107
National Conference on Cardiopulmonary Resuscitation and Emergency Care, 21

158

Copyright Acknowledgments